MW00879107

NICOLE REINA

The Law of Attraction is Incomplete, Part I – How to Leverage Consciousness to Unlock Your Manifesting Power

Overcome Limitation, End Frustration, and Finally Create the Life You Desire

First published by KDP 2024

Copyright © 2024 by Nicole Reina

Medical Disclaimer:

The information provided in this book is for educational and informational purposes only and is not intended as a substitute for professional medical advice, diagnosis, or treatment. The techniques, suggestions, and exercises outlined in this book, including muscle testing and detoxification practices, are based on the author's personal experience and research. Always consult with your healthcare provider before making any changes to your diet, health regimen, or wellness practices. The author and publisher are not responsible for any adverse effects or consequences resulting from the use of any suggestions, techniques, or practices described in this book.

General Disclaimer:

The information contained in this book is provided for educational and informational purposes only. While the author has made every effort to ensure the accuracy and reliability of the information, it is not intended as a substitute for professional advice, be it medical, legal, financial, or otherwise. Readers are encouraged to seek the advice of a qualified professional before implementing any suggestions or practices outlined in this book.

The techniques, strategies, and concepts discussed in this book are based on the author's personal experiences and research. Results may vary from person to person, and no outcomes are guaranteed. The author and publisher assume no liability for any actions taken by readers based on the information provided in this book. By reading this book, you agree that the author and publisher are not responsible for any adverse effects or consequences resulting from the use of any suggestions or techniques described.

First edition

ISBN (paperback): 979-8-34532-124-9
ISBN (hardcover): 979-8-34245-308-0

This book was professionally typeset on Reedsy.
Find out more at reedsy.com

To my beloved husband, John Reina.
You have believed in me since day one.
Thank you for your love, support
& unwavering faith.
Together, we move mountains.

To my wonderfully brilliant children,
Alex & Catalina Reina.
Thank you for always teaching me.

To my mom, Sharla Lee Shults.
Thank you for always being there
& picking me up when I fall.
I love having you with me.

To my mentor, Michael E. Connor.
Thank you for your knowledge,
immense patience
& unending generosity.
I owe you my life.

The Law of Attraction is powerful, but it is only one small part of the whole. As a predominant creator, true positive creation comes from aligning your consciousness with love.

Nicole Reina

Contents

Preface

At some point in life, we all yearn for change—whether it is attracting abundance, cultivating inner peace, or healing from past wounds. Many of us turn to the Law of Attraction and practice reciting affirmations, chanting mantras, and envisioning the life we desire. Yet, despite our best efforts, we often find ourselves back where we started, stuck in the same patterns.

Why does real, lasting change feel so elusive?

The answer lies in a part of ourselves that often remains hidden and unaddressed: the unconscious mind. This is where the Law of Attraction falls short—where it is incomplete. While it is powerful, most teachings overlook the deeper patterns within us that silently shape our reality.

For years, I experienced being trapped in a cycle. I would set goals, only to feel something invisible holding me back. I did not realize that deeply buried beliefs about myself and the world controlled every decision I made. The harder I pushed, the more resistance I encountered. I believed I needed to work harder, not realizing my unconscious mind was clinging to the past.

Then, in 2020, everything changed. After discovering the Law of Attraction, my life completely transformed, filled with moments I could only describe as miraculous. But after those magical moments, I faced frustration, turmoil, and challenges. It felt like the magic left me, like a light suddenly flickering out.

I soon realized the key to real change was not trying harder, but identifying the unconscious mind and recognizing the unconscious patterns shaping my life. These patterns—formed by past trauma and fears—kept me stuck.

Positive affirmations and meditation were not enough until I brought these patterns into conscious awareness.

Through this process, I experienced a miracle: the return of my hearing, something I had completely lost as a baby. I learned that my hearing loss was an emotional shield, a manifestation of my unconscious mind protecting me from the painful sounds of my inner and outer environments. Once I became conscious of my unprocessed emotions, my healing began.

This book is about diving deeper—beyond affirmations—into the unconscious mind, the part of us that drives behavior and shapes reality. Understanding how consciousness works is the missing piece in manifesting with ease. The unconscious mind holds the key.

Throughout the book, you will find alternating sections of reading and reflection. After each chapter, you will encounter powerful journaling prompts that expand on the themes discussed. These exercises will help you integrate new knowledge and reflect on how it affects you personally. You will have the space to uncover limiting beliefs, identify unconscious patterns, and release the resistance that has been holding you back.

This approach will allow you to absorb the material at a deeper level, moving beyond mere intellectual understanding and into personal transformation. It is not just about changing your thoughts. It is about raising your consciousness.

Together, we will explore the patterns shaping your life. Through journaling prompts and reflections, you will uncover limiting beliefs and fears. You will learn to recognize resistance as your unconscious mind's way of keeping you safe, and how to move through that resistance with compassion. This journey of life is not about survival. It is about thriving.

As you move through this book, approach each chapter with an open heart. Be gentle with yourself. Resistance means you are on the edge of transformation. Trust that by facing these unconscious patterns, you are not just surviving.

You are creating.

Let us walk this journey together, uncovering the patterns that have been hiding in the shadows for far too long. Together, we will bring them to light and transform them—one conscious choice at a time.

With love and gratitude,
   Nicole Reina

Acknowledgments

First and foremost, I would like to thank my family and children for staying by my side even through the darkest moments of this journey. Your love and patience helped me to continually learn, grow, and become the person I am today.

I would also like to express my deepest gratitude to my support group, Attracting Grace, and its founder Michael Connor, whose guidance, expertise, and support over these last several years were invaluable in shaping this book. I am grateful for the safe space, patience, love, and encouragement we provide for each other every day. Together, we are shaping humanity.

And last, but certainly not least, thank you to all of my teachers who have been there for me throughout my life. Some of you were friends, professional connections, acquaintances, and co-workers, while others were complete strangers. Each of you entered my life at the perfect time—every encounter was a holy encounter. At times, I was ready to listen and act on the wisdom you offered me. Other times, I was not in a place to recognize the Divine timing of your arrival or reappearance. Regardless, know that I love and appreciate you more than you could ever know.

To anyone I may have caused pain along the way, knowingly or unknowingly, I humbly ask for your forgiveness. My journey, like all of ours, has been full of learning and unlearning, and I am grateful for your grace and understanding.

Introduction

"The Law of Attraction is NOT Your Friend," - Abraham-Hicks

What is the Law of Attraction, really?

If you have never heard of the Law of Attraction, I am glad this book is your first encounter. If you are already familiar with or actively practicing it, you are in for an eye-opener. While many strive to share the truth about this law, what is often presented is only a partial truth. Some people overlook or misunderstand crucial aspects of manifestation.

So, what exactly is this law?

To some, it is an unchanging natural law of the Universe. To others, it is a theory, perhaps even rooted in pseudoscience. Regardless of where you stand, the Law of Attraction is one of twelve universal laws derived from collective consciousness and historical wisdom. At its core, it suggests that like attracts like.

In human terms, this means our thoughts—whether positive or negative—shape our life experiences. The idea is that similar energies attract each other, so the nature of our thoughts and emotions draws in corresponding experiences.

In simpler terms: think positively, and positive things will happen; think negatively, and you will attract negative outcomes. But...this is misleading. It is not your thoughts that create the attraction point.

We attract what we *are*, not what we *think* we are. When we try to get something different but do not become different, our attraction point stays the same and we can never get what we want. As Steve Maraboli, renowned speaker, bestselling author, and philanthropist, said, "Your life is a reflection. You do not get what you want, you get what you are. You gotta be it to see it" (Say & Say, 2020b).

Since we are energy, we must be in energetic alignment with our desire before we can see it. By "being it," you align yourself energetically with what you want to attract, making it easier for that reality to manifest.

Forbes Health quotes Christy Whitman, a certified Law of Attraction coach, who explains, "Thanks to Albert Einstein's famous equation, $E=mc^2$, we now understand that matter and energy are inseparable and that energy is the basis of everything in our tangible universe. Everything that manifests in the physical world does so by a process of resonant energies being drawn together" (Neumann, 2024b).

The Law of Attraction in Popular Culture

Over the past couple of decades, the Law of Attraction has gained significant popularity. What was once an obscure theory suddenly became mainstream, largely because of the success of the documentary *The Secret* by Rhonda Byrne (2006) and endorsements from celebrities like Oprah Winfrey, Lady Gaga, and Steve Harvey. These advocates praised the power of positive thinking, presenting it as a great secret finally being revealed to the world.

In theory, it sounds fantastic, right? Just change your thoughts, "feel" like you already have what you want, and it will magically appear in your life.

How delightful.

People created books and documentaries filled with anecdotal evidence, which seemed very convincing. This law enchanted many, including myself, who eagerly followed its principles. The burning question was, "Why not?"

But here is the thing: the Law of Attraction is NOT your friend, and it is not something magical. It is simply an invisible force that manages your experiences—whether you see them as good or bad.

But is it true?

There is no concrete scientific evidence proving the Law of Attraction exists. However, my personal experiences, along with those of millions of people around the world, suggest that it is real. The only way to know for sure is to try it for yourself. For the sake of this book, let us assume it is true.

What I am about to say might shock you, and it could be just a tad controversial.

In my humble opinion, the Law of Attraction really SUCKS!

Allow me to explain.

Why the Law of Attraction Sucks

There are two main reasons the Law of Attraction is challenging. First, you cannot turn it off. It is an absolute law. Imagine planting a strawberry seed. The seed will attract everything it needs to grow strawberries. It already knows what to do. It is an automatic process. If you decide to plant a different seed in the same spot, it will grow something else, because it is a different vibration.

Why is this a problem?

Everything you see and have in your life is a direct reflection of the Law of Attraction at work. Scientific studies, like the Matthew Effect, support this idea. The Matthew Effect describes how individuals accumulate social or economic success in proportion to their initial level of popularity, friends, and wealth. In simpler terms: the rich get richer, and the poor get poorer (*Matthew Effect*, n.d.). The Bible also mentions this principle in Matthew 25:29: "For everyone who possesses will be given more, and he will have an abundance. But the one who does not have, even what he has will be taken away from him" (*Matthew 25:29*, n.d.).

Why does this make the Law of Attraction suck? Because you cannot turn it off, you are always attracting something based on your emotions—whether or not you like it. It is always on, always working, always pulling from your emotions.

Second, and even more frustrating, is the fact that many of your thoughts are *unconscious*. This makes the Law of Attraction an incomplete idea. You cannot change your circumstances by just thinking about something different. It goes deeper than this. This is the part that supporters of the law often forget to mention, and it might be the source of any frustration you are experiencing in your life.

You do not have control over what you unconsciously create. Between the ages of zero and seven, a lot happened that shaped your life. Perhaps there was trauma, abuse, judgment, or scarcity. Or maybe you had a happy home but still struggled to meet expectations. Whatever your situation, these early experiences created emotions that triggered the Law of Attraction to form core beliefs. Most of this is unconscious, meaning it is working against you without you even realizing it.

The Baby Elephant and the Invisible Rope

Consider the story of a baby elephant. A baby elephant is tied to a small pole with a piece of rope. Each time the elephant tries to move, the rope holds him back. As the elephant grows into a powerful adult, he remains tied by the same small rope. He fails to realize he could easily break free; he accepts the limitation because it is all he has ever known.

In this metaphor, you are the elephant. You have grown strong, but an invisible rope is holding you back.

Here is another example. Imagine a train speeding at 250 mph in one direction. If the conductor wants to reverse the train, it is impossible to simply flip a switch. He must first slow the train, bring it to a complete stop, and then gradually start moving in the other direction. At first, the train moves slowly, but eventually, it gains momentum. Turning it around takes time.

The longer you have held on to a belief, the more powerful the Law of Attraction is at working against you. And since much of this is unconscious, it is unknown to you until it becomes conscious.

Experiencing the Law of Attraction

For many, the initial experience with the Law of Attraction feels magical. But with time, the magic can fade, leaving people frustrated, disappointed, and doubting whether the Law of Attraction is real.

Why does this happen? Were we duped? Is this law a scam? Is it something about us?

Suddenly, the Law of Attraction goes from being the next big thing to being labeled as dangerous pseudoscience. But those who have authentically experienced it know it is not pseudoscience—it is an authentic law. Science may not have proven it yet, but personal experience can be undeniable.

Take my story, for example. When I first discovered the Law of Attraction, I was searching for something different; something that would give my life more meaning. I had experienced trauma as a child and young adult and found it challenging to live the life I desired.

Despite these challenges, I had already accomplished a lot. I completed my MBA and started a company that is still in operation today. But I was under tremendous stress, and my health was suffering. I needed a change.

I began a meditation practice and was introduced to Abraham-Hicks. If you are unfamiliar with Abraham, it is a non-physical entity of consciousness channeled by Esther Hicks, focusing on teaching the Law of Attraction. I know this might sound a little "woo-woo" to some, but for me, the teachings were profound and resonated on a deep, personal level. After growing up with trauma and abuse, this information was life-changing and transformational.

After listening to Abraham's teachings, I experienced a real energetic shift and fell in love with the concept. The energy I felt was undeniable. Soon after, in mid-2020, my husband and I watched the documentary *The Secret* by Rhonda Byrne (2006), and we were both blown away. The information presented seemed so simple, so wonderful. We took a leap of faith and applied the principles in our daily lives.

We both experienced a profound shift that I can only describe as a spontaneous awakening. I suddenly had clarity on many things, including the Bible—a shocking revelation for me. Despite my Methodist upbringing, I identified as agnostic and rarely engaged in anything religious.

That the Bible crossed my mind, and that I understood it, blew me away. It was all metaphors, not to be taken literally, and I understood it all. I felt filled with love, warmth, and understanding as if I were being hugged by a higher power. I wanted to shout to the world, "God is real! It is the truth! Why does anyone not see this?!"

For weeks, I experienced pure bliss. Everywhere I went, I felt light. I loved everyone I saw at the core of my being, whether or not I knew them. In my mind, I would say "God bless you" over and over. It was surreal. I was far from the person I used to be—it was like I had taken a quantum leap into another reality, and I was enjoying every moment. Each day, I woke up grateful and genuinely excited to live my life.

Things manifested in incredible ways. Money appeared in large quantities, clients came effortlessly, bills worth thousands of dollars disappeared, and I felt incredibly empowered. It was as if nothing could bring me down, and I knew I could do anything. I was on top of the world.

Until I wasn't.

A few weeks into this experience, something changed. Out of the blue, I suddenly crashed. It felt like a light switch had turned off inside me, and all the previous sensations were gone.

The magic disappeared.

"God left me!" I sobbed uncontrollably. "He left me!"

I was in total shock and could not understand what had happened.

It was the most painful experience of my life. Shame, guilt, anger, and frustration overwhelmed me. A million unanswered questions plagued my mind. I broke down and cried for days. My mental illness symptoms returned.

As a child and young adult, I was diagnosed with depression and anxiety with bipolar tendencies. These symptoms had been gone for years, but they suddenly reappeared. I fell into a deep depression and struggled with bouts of rage and suicidal thoughts.

As high as my experience had been, I found myself at rock bottom, mentally and emotionally. I contemplated suicide multiple times. If not for my family and the support I received from my coach and mentor, I would not be here writing this book today.

This is why I am so passionate about sharing the knowledge I have gained so others can avoid repeating the same mistakes.

The Disillusioned Belief

The Law of Attraction is real, whether or not there is scientific evidence to support it. Once you experience the effects of its principles, it is undeniable. But there is a disillusioned belief that all you need to do is think positively and "feel" good to create a happy life. While there is some truth to this, it is only a half-truth.

Take the documentary *The Secret* by Rhonda Byrne (2006), for example. While some of the information presented is valid, many parts are very misleading and unclear.

For instance, in the documentary, Bob Proctor, a world-renowned speaker and Law of Attraction expert, claims, "This secret gives you everything you want—happiness, wealth, and health" (Byrne, 0:02:42). He also says, "Everything that is coming into your life, you are attracting into your life, and it is attracted by virtue of the images you are holding in your mind. It is what you are thinking" (Byrne, 0:04:42).

John Assaraf, a bestselling author, and entrepreneur, adds, "Our job as humans is to hold on to the thoughts that we want, make it absolutely clear in our minds what we want, and from that, we invoke one of the greatest laws in the universe, and that is the Law of Attraction. You become what you think about most, but you also attract what you think about most" (Byrne, 0:05:42).

These statements, while popular, are very misleading—especially to someone new to the concept. While the Law of Attraction starts with your thoughts, it is your emotions, not just thoughts, that truly determine what manifests. Thoughts are just thoughts until you choose to focus on them. This is where it gets tricky: the documentary does not mention a word about unconscious thoughts.

The truth is this: what we hold in mind, consciously or unconsciously, affects our lives under the Law of Attraction.

We have over 60,000 thoughts a day on average. It is impossible to monitor all of them or even know which ones to change. Later in the documentary, it is suggested that thoughts and feelings together create your life, but this is still a half-truth. Feelings are not the same as emotions, which I will address later in the book.

When people became disenchanted with the Law of Attraction, many asked Oprah Winfrey why she helped popularize something that seemed "bogus" and did not work. Oprah, who was instrumental in popularizing the Law of Attraction after Rhonda Byrne's *The Secret* (2006) came out, promoted the idea that what you focus on and visualize will manifest in your life. Her reply to the public in her show *The Oprah Winfrey Show* was that this was indeed one secret, but she admitted that many other secrets remain untaught (Winfrey, 2007).

Interesting, is it not? It is time we get the whole truth.

Why This Book is Different

The purpose of this book is not to cast doubt on the Law of Attraction, which I know from personal experience exists. Those who dismiss it as "bogus" or "woo-woo" simply do not understand the full scope of what it is about. While Abraham-Hicks offers valuable insights into the Law of Attraction, many people still experience misunderstanding that leads to frustration.

If this misunderstanding did not exist, more of us would consistently experience the joy and bliss the Law promises. The reality is that many people, including myself, have been mentally and physically affected by misguided beliefs, and some have even died by their own hands. This is a real problem, and I am passionate about teaching the higher truth.

My goal is to bridge the gap between what individuals experience in life and what they understand about the Law of Attraction. By doing so, I hope to help others end the frustration and finally create the life of their dreams.

The end result? Clarity and pure joy.

1

The Issue With "Thinking Positive"

"Negative thoughts are not inherently bad; they give positivity its meaning. By becoming aware and accepting them, you gain the power to choose differently. When you stop fighting and embrace this balance, life flows effortlessly."
— *Nicole Reina, Author, Facilitator, and Mindset Coach*

While positive thinking has its benefits, relying on it too heavily can turn it toxic, leading to harmful emotions and behaviors like shame, victimizing, blaming, and low self-esteem. A common misconception with the Law of Attraction is the belief that to create favorable outcomes, you must always think positively. While there is some truth to this, it is a flawed approach because it implies that negative thinking is inherently bad. This judgment creates fear and drives people to avoid pain, which ironically leads to even more pain.

In his book *Breaking the Habit of Being Yourself*, Dr. Joe Dispenza (2012), a neuroscientist, and bestselling author, explains, "We unconsciously live by a set of memorized behaviors, thoughts, and emotional reactions, all running like computer programs behind the scenes of our conscious awareness. That is why it is not enough to 'think positive,' because most of who we are might live subconsciously as negativity in the body" (p. 26).

But what happens if you believe that feeling bad is, well, bad?

In the documentary *The Secret*, it is suggested that if you feel good, you are creating a future aligned with your desires, and if you feel bad, you are doing the opposite. This oversimplification leads to the misconception that it is wrong to feel bad *(Byrne, 2006)*.

For me, this belief took root early in life as a direct consequence of trauma and abuse. I believed negative emotions were bad, so I never allowed myself to feel them. By burying my feelings and forcing a smile, I convinced myself that this was the way to find happiness. I even adopted a tough exterior to prevent others from getting angry or frustrated with me, which only added to my internal toxicity. I became a master at hiding my true feelings until they became completely unconscious to me.

This is why, when I suddenly filled myself with positive energy, all the negativity I had suppressed had to come out. I had buried so much that all I needed was one small trigger to completely overwhelm me, leading to a total crash, both emotionally and physically. There has to be balance; for the good to come in, the "bad" must be released.

The Importance of Embracing Negative Emotions

There is nothing wrong with having negative thoughts or feeling bad. In fact, it is a necessary component of living. It is crucial to accept these emotions as a natural part of life. Without negative emotions, we can never truly appreciate what is good. Just as we need sadness to fully value happiness, or failure to recognize success, life's contrasts give meaning to our experiences.

For example, overcoming challenges at work makes achievements more rewarding, and experiencing loss deepens our gratitude for what we have. This is the entire purpose of the dualistic world we live in. To know and appreciate light, we must first experience darkness. The balance between opposites is what shapes our growth and helps us to find greater fulfillment in both the highs and the lows.

During my recovery, anger was the emotion I struggled with the most. When I felt angry, I would become even angrier because I was frustrated with myself for feeling that way. And, of course, the more I focused on anger, the more the Law of Attraction caused this emotion to expand. It was a vicious cycle.

Then, one day, my 12-year-old daughter said something that changed everything for me:

"Mom, you need to normalize anger."

I hugged her so tight, realizing how right she was.

Avoiding negative thoughts or emotions by forcing positivity will backfire. Your body needs to be in balance energetically. It is impossible to eliminate all negativity because, for every positive, there must be a negative—this is the Law of Polarity. The core of this law is that everything in the universe has a counterpart, and these opposites are not in conflict but are interconnected parts of a unified whole.

For example, using affirmations to avoid pain can be problematic. While affirmations are powerful, they are not meant to be used as a shield against negative emotions. If we do not allow ourselves to feel bad out of fear of creating negative circumstances, our affirmations become toxic because they lack authenticity.

Another common pitfall is the constant search for negative thoughts or beliefs to replace with positive ones, hoping to create a desired outcome. The challenge here lies in the fact that our minds are filled with countless negative thoughts, making it impossible to change them all. Theoretically, if you have 60,000 thoughts a day, 30,000 of them will be negative.

This means you could spend forever replacing negative thoughts with positive ones seeing no actual results. You are just shifting things around, driven by fear, and ultimately creating more of what you do not want. This approach is toxic and leads to frustration and low self-esteem because the desired outcome never materializes.

The Power of Acceptance and Focus

Accepting a negative situation, thought, or emotion as it is and then choosing to shift your attention to something positive is a very different strategy from resisting negative emotions and forcing yourself to think positively all the time. The former approach fosters a compassionate state of being, while the latter denies authenticity, leading to frustration, guilt, and a diminished sense of self.

It all comes down to focus and choice. You always have the power to choose where to direct your thoughts. However, when a belief becomes unconscious, you may not even be aware of its presence until something brings it to the surface.

Taking action is what truly creates change. It is the necessary step for manifestation. Dreaming, thinking, and feeling good are all parts of the equation, but action is what brings them to life. However, it must be the right action.

When you hold a thought long enough, it becomes a belief. This belief leads to an emotion, which then drives the actions you take. The Law of Attraction is the force that creates emotion and propels you to act. The action you take leads to an experience, which then reinforces the original belief, starting the cycle all over again. This cycle is known as the belief cycle. It will continue until you choose to break it by making different choices.

Feeling vs. Emotion: Understanding the Difference

It is important to understand that feeling is not the same as emotion, though many sources teaching the Law of Attraction often confuse the two. I often refer to the documentary *The Secret* by Rhonda Byrne because it is one of the most popular and widely viewed documentaries on the Law of Attraction today. It is also what impacted my life the most, and is one of the most misguided and incomplete sources out there. The film suggests that your thoughts and feelings create your life, and implies that when you "feel good," you attract good things.

In *The Secret* documentary, Joe Vitale, a prominent author, says, "It is really important that you feel good because this feeling good is what goes out as a signal to the universe and starts to attract more of itself to you" (Byrne, 2006, 0:20:37). Unfortunately, this is not entirely accurate and misses a key concept.

Another way to understand the difference between feeling and emotions by comparing emotions to the engine of a car, driving our actions, while feelings are like the car's body, giving shape to our experiences. In other words, feelings are what we label emotions to be based on our perception. An emotion is a manifestation of thought and is the engine of the Law of Attraction.

If we decide to "feel" happy, the thoughts propelled by the Law of Attraction will generate more thoughts that "feel" happy until we express the emotion that is eventually manifested. Emotions are the sensations or the end result of what we consistently hold in mind. It is the energy generated when we think enough thoughts to create it. Once we put a label on what we feel, it changes the nature of the emotion.

Here is the kicker. You can consciously feel good while unconsciously feeling bad, and not even realize it. The Law of Attraction does not just respond to the thoughts you consciously expand upon; it also responds to the momentum created by your emotions, which manifest as sensations in the body. You might label these feelings as "good" or "bad," but it is the emotion behind them that drives manifestation.

Here is an example from an article in Psychology Today: Imagine you are at a party and notice a tightening in your stomach and shallow breathing. You might label this feeling as "awkwardness" because you do not know many people there, or you just saw an ex-partner. But another person might label the same sensations as "excitement" because they enjoy meeting new people or are eager to reconnect with their ex (Allyn, 2022).

What you label the feeling affects how the Law of Attraction expands upon your thoughts, generating more thoughts that match, which eventually creates an emotion. This emotion is the gas pedal for manifestation, leading to a particular experience.

It is not the thought itself, but your perspective of the thought that creates the emotion you feel. Let us revisit the earlier example:

- If you label the feeling as negative (awkward), and continue to focus on that thought, it eventually solidifies and manifests as the emotion of awkwardness. The Law of Attraction then expands on this emotion, likely leading to a negative experience—unless you become aware of it, accept it, and consciously shift your focus. By shifting your focus, you can change the experience.

- If someone else labels the same sensations as positive (excited), the emotion that develops could be enthusiasm, eagerness, or anticipation. The Law of Attraction will expand on these emotions, leading to a more positive experience. This person is likely to have a great time at the party.

Emotions are essentially the body's reaction to the mind, which creates stories based on past experiences or future fears. But things are not always what they seem, and our judgments can distort the truth. Instead of labeling experiences negatively, we can accept them and choose to create the emotions we wish to feel.

Becoming Emotionally Intelligent

Before we dive into becoming emotionally intelligent, if you are someone like me, you may wonder what this even means. We are most likely very familiar with the broad term "intelligence," but what does it mean to be "emotionally intelligent"?

According to an article in Psychology Today,

"Emotional intelligence refers to the ability to identify and manage one's own emotions, as well as the emotions of others. It is generally said to include a few skills: namely emotional awareness, or the ability to identify and name one's own emotions; the ability to harness those emotions and apply them to tasks like thinking and problem solving; and the ability to manage emotions, which includes both regulating one's own emotions when necessary and helping others to do the same" (*The Roots of Emotional Intelligence*, n.d.).

When we develop emotional intelligence and practice self-compassion, we are better equipped to use the Law of Attraction to our advantage and improve our experiences. As Abraham-Hicks says, "The manifestation of the stuff follows precisely the manifestation of the emotion. That is why we want so much for you to make the manifestation of the emotion, not just your main event, but the only event that you are focused upon" (Dimas, 2020).

Here is an important question: If the Law of Attraction matches you to the frequency at which you are vibrating through your emotional state, how can you know where you are vibrating without going through experiences, especially if you are unaware of the emotion you are feeling?

The answer lies in understanding your level of consciousness. This awareness is the key to unlocking the true power of the Law of Attraction and creating the life you desire.

2

Introspective Reflection

"Remind yourself that you cannot fail at being yourself."
— *Wayne Dyer*

A s you reflect on the insights from the previous chapter about the limitations of positive thinking, recall moments when trying to 'stay positive' may have unintentionally created obstacles. Examining these experiences can offer valuable clarity on how a more balanced approach might serve you better.

Before moving on to Chapter Three, take a moment to engage with the following questions. Journal your responses to deepen your understanding and integrate these insights into your journey. Write in this book or a personal journal.

Journal Prompts

1. Reflect on a time when you felt pressured to "stay positive" in a challenging situation. What were the outcomes, both positive and negative, and how did the experience make you feel?

Then, consider how shifting to gratitude, rather than just positive thinking, might provide a clearer, more productive mindset. For instance, imagine someone facing health challenges. Initially, they might feel frustration or worry, but by focusing on gratitude, they could say, "I am grateful for the strength my body has shown me through this experience and for the opportunity to learn more about how to take care of myself." This shift can open up a sense of calm and a more balanced perspective.

Write your thoughts.

_____

_____

_____

_____

_____

_____

_____

_____

_____

_____

_____

_____

_____

_____

_____

_____

_____

_____

_____

_____

_____

_____

_____

_____

_____

_____

_____

_____

_____

_____

2. "Thinking positively" differs from practicing gratitude or appreciation. When challenges arise, shifting to gratitude can help you navigate them with a clearer, more productive mindset. For example, someone who has lost a job may initially feel panic or fear, but by leaning on faith and expressing gratitude—such as saying, "I am grateful for what I learned in that role; it helped me grow, and those skills will serve me in the future"—they can find calm and openness to new possibilities.

Take a moment to reflect on a challenge you are currently facing or have faced in the past. Write words of gratitude or appreciation for this experience. How has it helped you grow, and what lessons can you carry forward? Finally, consider how practicing gratitude might change the way you approach similar challenges in the future.

Write your thoughts.

_____

_____

_____

_____

_____

_____

_____

_____

_____

_____

_____

_____
_____
_____
_____
_____
_____
_____
_____

3. Take a moment to reflect on this quote: "You can never get to peace and inner security without first acknowledging all of the good things in your life. If you are forever wanting and longing for more without first appreciating things the way they are, you will stay in discord." — _Doc Childre and Howard Martin_

Now, if you choose, declare the following intention: _"For today and moving forward from this point, I choose to have an 'attitude of gratitude' that carries me through my day."_

Next, list the blessings that are present in your life right now. If this feels challenging, start small—write simple things like your home, your bed, your pillow, your family, your pet(s), or even your toothbrush. Remember, many people lack basic necessities. In fact, if you have food in your fridge, clothes on your back, a roof over your head, and a place to sleep, you are richer than 75% of the world. And since you are reading this book, you are more blessed than almost one billion people who cannot read.

Write your blessings below.

_____
_____
_____
_____
_____
_____
_____

3

Consciousness Determines Your Reality

"Yesterday I was clever, so I wanted to change the world. Today I
am wise, so I am changing myself."
— *Rumi, a 13th-century Persian Poet, Mystic, and Sufi Philosopher.*

C onsciousness is the state or quality of being aware—whether it is
awareness of the world around you or something within yourself.
It is described often as sentience, self-awareness, or the ability to
experience and feel. In simpler terms, consciousness makes you "you" and
allows you to interact with the world and your inner self.

Without diving too deeply into the science, it is crucial to understand that
consciousness plays a foundational role in shaping your reality. While the Law
of Attraction amplifies your thoughts and emotions, it is your consciousness
that gives rise to those thoughts in the first place.

This is where we go deeper than the Law of Attraction, and it is another
reason the Law of Attraction is incomplete. Your level of consciousness
determines the range of thoughts available to you, which are also influenced
by your emotional state. As your emotional state improves, so does your

consciousness. While the Law of Attraction remains constant, you have the power to elevate your consciousness, and this power enables you to change your thoughts automatically.

Here is the key difference: Different levels of consciousness change the nature of your thoughts, while the Law of Attraction simply amplifies whatever thoughts and emotions your current level of consciousness generates. Becoming aware of your consciousness gives you insight into the vibrational signals you send out, influencing what you attract.

Your inner experience, shaped by your current level of consciousness, directly influences your outer reality. In my experience, the quickest way to transform your life is not just by thinking positively or focusing on feeling good—it is by raising your current level of consciousness.

The Power of Consciousness

As mentioned earlier, the Law of Attraction magnifies your emotional frequency, which affects your experiences. Sometimes, these experiences can be uncomfortable or even painful. Typically, the most common way to gauge your vibration is by tuning into your emotional state. However, for many people—especially those who have experienced trauma—identifying emotions can be challenging.

So, what if there was a shortcut?

What if you could know where you are vibrating at any moment, or what frequencies you are sending out to the universe, without having to endure painful experiences first?

What if you could understand what you were unconsciously attracting without going through difficult situations?

Consciousness Divided into Three Parts

Think of consciousness as a multifaceted diamond—it is complex, but when broken down, it becomes easier to understand. Psychologists like Freud and Carl Jung have described these aspects in various ways, but let's simplify them like a three-layered cake, where each layer represents a different part of your mind:

1. **Super-Conscious:** The "top" layer, your connection to higher wisdom or your "inner genius." It is the source of your best ideas and deep insights, embodying the highest field of information that exists.
2. **Self-Conscious:** The middle layer, where your everyday thoughts live. This is the rational part of your ego, responsible for making decisions and planning for the future. It drives your desires for a good life, whether that means financial success, fulfilling relationships, or personal growth.
3. **Unconscious (or Subconscious):** The foundation, or bottom layer. It operates automatically, controlling habits like riding a bike. Focused on survival, this part can resist change and trigger feelings like shame, guilt, or frustration when it senses a threat.

It is interesting to note that according to scientific research, our unconscious mind controls 95% of our thoughts and behaviors, leaving only 5% to conscious awareness. This means most of our decisions and actions are automatic. Insights from cognitive neuroscience and experts like Dr. Bruce Lipton underscore the unconscious's powerful role in shaping our reality (Lipton, 2012; Blias, 2021). By understanding and harnessing these layers of consciousness, you can move beyond the Law of Attraction alone, achieving deeper self-awareness and greater rewards in life.

Now, back to the earlier question: What if there was a way to know where you are vibrating or what frequencies you are sending out to the universe without having to experience something first? And what if you could understand what you were unconsciously vibrating?

Is this possible? Get ready—this could change your life.

It is possible. Consciousness is 100% measurable.

Measuring Consciousness With muscle testing

By using muscle testing, a method of applied kinesiology, you can measure your own emotional frequency, or level of consciousness. This technique is popular among chiropractors, acupuncturists, and sports medicine practitioners who use it to identify stressors, blockages, and potential health issues.

Here is the exciting part: with muscle testing, you can check the emotional frequency of many other things you may not have thought of, such as people, places, philosophies, movies, books, and even music.

By doing this, you have the potential to know what you are attracting—*before you attract it!*

Think of your body as a guide, directing you toward truth and alignment.

Here is how muscle testing works:

1. **Setup**: Muscle testing requires two people—a tester and a subject.
2. **Position**: The subject holds either their left or right arm straight out.
3. **Focus**: The subject holds a specific thought, looks at an image, or makes a statement for a yes or no answer.
4. **Application**: Using two fingers, the tester applies gentle downward pressure to the subject's arm.
5. **Interpretation**: If the arm remains strong, it is an affirmative or "yes" response. If the arm weakens, it suggests a negative response.

This simple yet powerful tool can be used to help reveal unconscious beliefs that might be holding you back. By regularly using muscle testing, you can make conscious choices that align with your true desires, enhancing the effectiveness of the Law of Attraction.

Self-muscle testing: The Sway Test

When you are on your own, self-muscle testing is a practical way to tap into your body's intuitive responses. Many of my clients have found the Sway Test to be the easiest method to use. Here are the steps:

1. **Position Yourself**: Stand with arms relaxed, feet shoulder-width apart, and toes pointing forward. If seated, keep your spine straight and feet flat.
2. **Relax**: Allow your body to relax and move naturally without controlling any movement or the outcome.
3. **Intend to Get the Truth**: Approach the test with the intention of uncovering the truth, whatever it may be.
4. **Make a Statement**: Make a statement that you know is true such as "My name is [Your Name]." Observe if your body leans forward (true) or backward (false).
5. **Practice**: Test with false statements ("I am an insect") to understand your body's responses.
6. **Explore**: Once familiar, use the Sway Test on any statement or decision.

Muscle testing tunes into your body's wisdom. This allows you to truly discern between what is good for your body, and what is not, making this a truly empowering tool for everyday decisions.

For a visual of what the Sway Test looks like, see Appendix II at the end of this chapter.

Muscle testing and the Emotional Scale by Dr. David Hawkins

You might not have heard this before. Your mind cannot tell the difference between truth and falsehood. It simply creates stories based on the past. Your "gut instinct" is influenced by your ego, which is also rooted in the past and is not the same as intuition. The lower chakras govern your gut instinct, while the higher chakras guide your intuition. The primitive part of the brain, often called the "reptilian brain," triggers instinctive reactions to danger.

Muscle testing operates on the premise that "the body does not lie." The body follows the mind, but it always vibrates at a certain frequency. Unlike the mind, the body cannot make stories or reason with anything. It simply reads things as they are. Using muscle testing, we can determine where the body is vibrating on an emotional frequency scale, as defined by Dr. David Hawkins. We can also discern whether something is life-giving or life-draining. For more in-depth information on this scale, you may refer to Dr. David R. Hawkins' book *The Map of Consciousness Explained (2020)*.

When performing a test using muscle testing, the body naturally benefits from life-giving substances, which strengthen it and therefore give a "yes" or strong response. Substances that are un-beneficial or life-taking weaken the body and therefore give a "no" answer or weak response when tested. What is good for one person may not be good for another, making this a powerful tool for individual discernment. Those with food allergies or health concerns can greatly benefit from this practice.

By using muscle testing to make choices that resonate with your body, you automatically raise your level of consciousness, which also increases your body's vibration or frequency—with no need to change a single thought. As your consciousness rises, so does the frequency of your thoughts. Since the Law of Attraction expands on whatever matches your vibration, increasing your consciousness leads to more positive experiences.

Who is Dr. David R. Hawkins?

Dr. David R. Hawkins, a renowned psychiatrist, spiritual teacher, and author, dedicated over 29 years of his life to studying and understanding the consciousness of humans. His work led him to discover and develop truly innovative methods for understanding and measuring consciousness. With this discovery, he bridged the gap of discerning truth from the falsehood that was so prevalent in humanity. As mentioned previously, the mind cannot tell the difference between truth and falsehood, and this has created many issues in people, countries, and even entire civilizations.

In his book, *The Eye of the Eye*, Dr. Hawkins (2016) says "Literally hundreds of millions of people throughout time have been destroyed for lack of a simple technique to overcome the mind's incapacity to tell a sheep from a wolf in sheep's clothing. Whole nations have gone down; whole civilizations have died from following propaganda, slogans, and belief systems that, when muscle tested, make one go weak. Although the muscle testing technique may sound simple and crude, so was the discovery of the lodestone for use as a compass" (Hawkins, p. 78).

Dr. Hawkins's first experience with consciousness came when he was a paperboy in the year 1939. In his book *I: Reality and Subjectivity* (Hawkins, 2014), he described his experience as follows:

"As a paperboy with a seventeen-mile bicycle route in rural Wisconsin, I was caught on a dark winter's night miles from home in a twenty-below-zero blizzard. The bicycle fell over on the ice and the fierce wind ripped the newspapers out of the handlebar basket, blowing them across the ice-covered, snowy field. There were tears of frustration and exhaustion and my clothes were frozen stiff. To get out of the wind, I broke through the icy crust of a high snow bank, dug out a space, and crawled into it. Soon the shivering stopped and there was a delicious warmth and then a state of peace beyond all description. This was accompanied by a suffusion of light and a presence of infinite love that had no beginning and no end and was undifferentiated from my essence. The physical body and surroundings faded as awareness was fused with this all-present, illuminated state. The mind grew silent; all thought stopped. An Infinite Presence was all that was or could be, beyond all time or description" (p. 20).

Dr. Hawkins told no one of his experience, because there was truly no one to understand, as he barely understood it himself. He went on with his life, and by the time he was 38, he became very ill. When he knew he was about to die, he experienced a miraculous recovery that sparked his inquisition into the realms of consciousness, later developing what would be his most notable contribution, a map that marked a scale of consciousness that ranked various levels and frequencies of human emotion, from shame to enlightenment (Hawkins, 2014, p. 20). This framework created an understanding of how different states of consciousness impact our lives and the ability to manifest desires.

How Dr. Hawkins Used muscle testing

Testing the Body's Response: Dr. Hawkins utilized muscle testing to observe how the body reacted to various statements or stimuli. By doing so, he could determine the emotional frequency of different thoughts and beliefs, helping individuals align their consciousness for more positive outcomes.

Discerning Consciousness Levels: Dr. Hawkins developed a scale that charted the levels of consciousness, with this scale containing a range of emotions ranging from 1 to 1,000. The scale correlates each emotional frequency to a level of being, which is another method of discerning vibration or frequency.

At each level, a different emotion highlights the spiritual state or vibration. Shame, for example, is very low on the scale and a negative vibration while love, bliss, and enlightenment are higher up. For example, when a statement like "I am unworthy" is muscle tested, it may produce a weak response or "no" answer in the body, showing a low vibrational state. Conversely, a statement like "I am beautiful" might produce an affirmative response, which would show a higher level of consciousness, hence a higher vibratory frequency.

Using muscle testing to Discern Truth: According to Dr. Hawkins, muscle testing (kinesiology) could discern truth from falsehood in almost anything. When testing something for yourself, use the statement "This XX is of my body's highest and best good" or even "This XX is good for my body." To ensure reliability, muscle testing is performed as a statement rather than a question. muscle testing only gives yes or no answers. The XX could be a personal decision, a belief, a book, a movie, a song or music, a business decision, a meeting with a person, a telephone call, a thought, an idea, a spiritual teaching, a teacher, etc. The list is endless.

- The reason this works is that the body does not think, it just is. It bypasses the conscious mind, which ego and subjective experience can influence.

Practical Application

Personal Growth: You can use muscle testing to identify limiting beliefs or negative emotions that might hold you back. This allows uncovering unconscious blocks that the Law of Attraction is responding to as it brings it to conscious awareness. Becoming conscious of it allows you to release it, improving your level of consciousness and raising your vibration.

Decision Making: Making decisions can be challenging, and muscle testing aids in making decisions that are positive for your experience. This is a wonderful tool for anyone struggling with indecision, which is often fueled by fear. You could test your body's response to a particular food or supplement, or even to a potential job offer to discern whether it aligns with your highest good.

Spiritual Development: muscle testing can enhance your spiritual practice and allow for major growth. It can discern the actual level of truth of spiritual practices, teachings, or ideas, which guides you to a higher consciousness and a happier life.

Learning muscle testing and Using it Effectively

1. **Choose your method:** muscle testing can either be done with a partner or adapted for self-testing. Choose a method that resonates with you. In my experience, I have found that self-testing offers the best benefit, as it allows you to do it anywhere you are (which is everywhere). Using a partner may limit you to certain times you are both available.

2. **Get the Basics:** To start, you must learn the basic techniques of muscle testing. Find a coach, or do your research online. Then, practice, practice, practice! First, test simple statements that you know are true or false to see how your body responds. This allows you to begin the trust process, which is necessary for this to work. For example, say your name out loud and see if you get a positive response from one of the testing methods, i.e.

arm stays strong with a tester or body leans forward with the sway test. Follow this by saying something untrue, like a different name or "I am a cat" and check if your arm goes weak with a tester or leans backward with the sway test.

3. **Everyday Life Application:** Do the basics until you are comfortable with the technique of your choice and know your body's response to stimuli or statements. Then, begin testing your response to thoughts, foods, supplements, medicines, books, magazines, music, and movies. I tell my clients to test anything that goes in their mouth, their eyes, and their ears. This means anything you eat, drink, or take orally, anything you watch or read, and anything you listen to. Have fun with it!

4. **Everything has energy, and everything is vibrating:** This means everything has the potential to lower or raise your vibrational frequency! It might surprise you to find out that a "good movie," "good book," or "healthy food" can weaken your body because its energy is determined by the intent behind the creation.

5. **Study Dr. Hawkins' Work:** Understanding consciousness requires study. Deepen your understanding by reading Dr. Hawkins' books. I would recommend starting with his book *Power vs Force* then *The Map of Consciousness Explained.* Both works do a great job of providing detailed explanations of his methods and how they relate to life application and spiritual growth. He has other works as well that you may find beneficial for your growth.

6. **Seek Guidance:** If you are new to muscle testing (kinesiology), you may wish to work with a practitioner or coach who is experienced in Dr. Hawkins' work. Not only can they guide you in learning the technique, but they can help you with applying it effectively in your life. It is important to learn this technique properly to ensure maximum benefit.

Understanding Intent

Have you ever wondered why your mom's or grandma's cooking often tastes better than your own? It is not just about the recipe—it is about the love they put into it. When they cook, they are not just fulfilling a chore; they are caring for their loved ones, pouring their love into every dish. This loving intention can change the energy of the food, making it taste better. Love and gratitude are powerful forces, and they can elevate anything, even the simplest meal.

Now, think about why some people bless their food before eating. Maybe you do it because it is a tradition or something your parents taught you. But blessing food goes beyond just a habit; it has a purpose. When you bless your food, you are raising its energetic frequency or keeping it aligned with the love that was put into preparing it. You are focusing on love and gratitude, which differs from the intent of eating just to fill your stomach.

Next time you are at a restaurant, try blessing your food. Restaurants often prepare food intending to make money, which can give the food a lower energetic frequency. By blessing it, you infuse it with positive energy, which can benefit your body and raise your frequency. It as a simple and powerful practice: just close your eyes and send love and gratitude to your food.

Tip: Before you order, check the energetic frequency of your food. You can use a method of muscle testing and make a statement to yourself, "This dish has a positive energy that is good for me" (Y/N). Trust the answer you receive. You can do the same with the restaurant itself: "Eating at this restaurant (name) is in my highest and best good" (Y/N). This practice helps you ensure that you are making choices that align with your well-being.

This idea applies to more than just food. Think about the books you read or the movies you watch. The intention behind their creation matters. A book or movie made just to make money might carry a lower energy than one created with love or pure intent. The first might lower your mood or mindset, while the second can uplift you. Your level of consciousness shapes the thoughts you think and the experiences you attract. When you surround yourself with high-energy creations, you invite positive experiences into your life.

You can even check the energy of a book or movie before you dive in using a muscle testing method. Make a statement to yourself such as "This book or movie has a positive impact on me" (Y/N). Using muscle testing puts your intuition to work. Let your intuition guide you to choices that elevate your life.

Dr. David Hawkins and Measuring Consciousness

Dr. Hawkins' most notable work, as mentioned earlier, was the development of a scale that charted different levels of consciousness using emotional frequencies with values ranging from 1 to 1,000 (Hawkins, 1998). Emotions like guilt, apathy, grief, fear, desire, anger, and pride fall below 200 on the scale, indicating lower states of consciousness that hinder personal growth and attract unwanted experiences.

Dr. Hawkins (1998) considers the level of 200 as the line of demarcation (p. 85). It is where fear ends and spirit, or love, begins. Emotions like courage, willingness, acceptance, reason, and love fall above 200, which represent more constructive and higher states of consciousness. Life's challenges become easier to handle at these levels.

Above 500 are the highest states, including joy, peace, gratitude, bliss, and enlightenment, which are associated with profound spiritual awakening.

Muscle testing and the Law of Attraction: What is the Link?

Let's revisit how muscle testing (kinesiology) connects with the Law of Attraction now that we understand consciousness, its role, and how it is measured. As discussed earlier, the Law of Attraction magnifies your emotional frequency, shaping your life experiences. When your consciousness is low, you are holding onto negative energy, which the Law of Attraction expands. Conversely, when your consciousness is high, the Law of Attraction amplifies higher frequencies, drawing more positive experiences into your life.

The challenge arises from the unconscious thoughts and emotions we all carry, which remain hidden until they surface through our experiences. By measuring your level of consciousness, you gain instant insight into where you are vibrating on the emotional scale, giving you a clear picture of what is coming your way before it manifests. The Law of Attraction is always at work, so would it not be useful to know what you are attracting before it becomes your reality?

Using muscle testing to assess your current emotional state (or consciousness) offers a direct way to understand what you are attracting and expanding through the Law of Attraction. It is a tool that reveals the thoughts and emotions your body is responding to, both consciously and unconsciously. By bringing unconscious patterns to light, you can shift your energy without the need to dissect your thoughts or feelings. Just as you step on a scale to check your weight, you can calibrate your energy to see what you are attracting. Since muscle testing provides data without judgment, you receive pure, accurate insights that can genuinely impact your life.

Consider this in terms of money. Suppose you state, "My level of consciousness (LOC) regarding money on a scale of 1-1000 using Dr. Hawkins' emotional frequency scale is over 200" (Y/N). If the response is no, it means you are attracting scarcity instead of abundance. You are on a path to experience less financial flow, which you probably would not have known without calibrating! This awareness gives you a chance to examine your thoughts without judgment and choose higher, more positive thoughts.

For a deeper dive into how to calibrate your level of consciousness on specific topics, I recommend Dr. David Hawkins' book *Power vs. Force*. He details the process, noting that it is most accurate when the tester approaches it with clinical detachment (Hawkins, 1998, p. 80). The book provides an example of how to proceed, particularly when someone's LOC is under 200.

Here is an example of testing your LOC or someone else's:

Start by stating, "My (or [person's name]) level of consciousness (LOC) regarding money on a scale of 1-1000, using Dr. Hawkins' emotional frequency scale calibrates over 200 (Y/N)."

If the answer is no, continue checking by increasing numbers until you get a yes. A quick way to do this is to check in increments of 20 at first, then narrow it down by checking in increments of 10, and finally by 1.

For example, if the LOC is under 200, start by checking "over 20," "over 40," and so on until you get a no. If you get a no at "over 40," it means the LOC is between 20 and 40. Then, check "over 30." If you get a yes at "over 30," continue with "over 31," "over 32," and so forth until you find the exact level.

Once you have identified the level, refer to the emotional scale in Appendix I to find the corresponding emotion. For example, if the LOC related to money is 35, it aligns with the emotion of blame, which falls within the range of guilt. At this level, you are likely attracting experiences that lead to guilt and self-blame, rather than positive outcomes. In this state, money slips away.

The Law of Attraction amplifies this effect, so the lower your consciousness level, the more challenging and painful your financial experiences become. To attract money more effectively, your LOC relative to the subject of money needs to be at 200 or higher. The higher you are on the scale, the easier it becomes to draw money into your life, as the Law of Attraction expands your positive experiences with increasing power.

Requirements to Ensure Test Accuracy

Now, as Dr. Hawkins (1998) explains in his book *Power vs Force*, there are requirements for accurate test results. He states:

"The best attitude is of clinical detachment. There are some people, however, who are incapable of a scientific, detached attitude and unable to be objective, and for whom the kinesiologic method will therefore not be accurate. Dedication and intention to the truth have to be given priority over personal opinions and trying to prove them as being "right."" (p. 80)

He then goes on to say, "The test is accurate only if the test subjects themselves calibrate over 200 and the intention of the use of the test is integrous, calibrating over 200. The requirement is one of detached objectivity and alignment with truth rather than subjective opinion. Thus, to try to prove a point negates accuracy. Approximately 10% of the population is not able to use the kinesiologic testing technique for as yet unknown reasons. Sometimes married couples, also for reasons as yet undiscovered, are unable to use each other as test subjects and may have to find a third person to be a test partner." (p.80).

If your overall LOC is below 200, just deciding and intending to use muscle testing (kinesiology) to measure your level of consciousness can potentially raise it above 200. Interestingly, the very act of deciding to use muscle testing calibrates at 437 on the emotional frequency scale, which aligns with the range of reason and the emotion of understanding.

Disqualification

There are also situations where disqualification occurs. In his book *Power vs Force*, Dr. Hawkins (1998) states that "Both skepticism (calibrates at 160) and cynicism calibrate below 200 because they reflect negative prejudgment. In contrast, true inquiry requires an open mind and honesty devoid of intellectual vanity. Negative studies of behavioral kinesiology all calibrate below 200 (usually at 160), as do the investigators themselves" (p.81).

My Experience of Real Miracles from Conscious Awareness

When you choose to work with consciousness, it is important to have a coach. A coach can help you see your blind spots—those unconscious aspects of yourself that you might not recognize without going through many painful experiences. Working with a coach allows you to achieve greater success and personal growth than you would on your own. The return on investment goes beyond monetary gain, affecting every aspect of your life, including relationships, career, health, and more.

You are worth investing in yourself.

When I experienced that incredible and sudden shift in my life that I call my "spontaneous awakening" followed by the mental and emotional crash, I knew I needed unconventional methods to heal painful aspects of myself. Traditional medicine would not help me, and the idea of being institutionalized was out of the question. I discovered the power of Reiki and soon met my mentor, Mike Connor, of Attracting Grace and the Magical Mind. He introduced me to muscle testing and showed me how I was creating my suffering—and how I could use this technique to improve my life.

Within a week of trying muscle testing, I was hooked. It was clear my body knew exactly what it needed. Because I was open to new possibilities, I could use it effectively and see immediate results. My decision-making changed completely. I used muscle testing to guide choices in my business, relationships, food, books, shows, and even social interactions. If my body said no, I declined the experience without fear, and totally without guilt or shame.

It was incredibly empowering to trust myself in this way—something that everyone deserves. Fear serves no one, and muscle testing provides a way to distinguish between fear and true guidance.

Although I faced challenges and had to learn new ways of doing things, my growth was steady. I began experiencing moments of pure happiness that I had thought were lost forever. My health improved, my marriage of two decades began to heal, my finances stabilized, and my business thrived. My life was finally turning around for the better.

I eventually became a Mindset Coach—something I once thought was impossible. I have since helped hundreds of clients achieve their dreams. My mother and I have reconciled a strained relationship, and we have been on this journey together for three years now. We are closer than ever, and we are in the midst of creating a mother-daughter coaching practice to help others find closure and new beginnings.

These are all miracles in their own right, but one stands out above the rest.

A Personal Miracle: Restoring My Hearing

I grew up with profound hearing loss. Diagnosed at 18 months, I was 98% deaf, mute, and labeled mentally handicapped. While I overcame the last two challenges—learning to speak perfectly and proving my mental capabilities— I remained hearing challenged, with just 2% hearing and the help of hearing aids.

If I had one lifelong desire, it was to hear. I went to great lengths to hide my disability and appear "normal" because that was what my step-father expected of me. It was instilled in me at such a young age that I latched onto it as absolute truth. I even developed internalized ableism to survive in a world that values hearing. For those who do not know, ableism refers to the idea that being "able-bodied" is the normal way to be, while anything different is abnormal.

I honestly could not understand why anyone would not want to hear, and I dreamed of one day being "normal," which surely meant I was chasing an impossible desire. Then, one day, everything changed.

Before this turning point, someone recommended that I read *Heal Your Body* by Louise Hay (1988), which presents an innovative approach linking negative thoughts and unresolved emotions with physical ailments. The book offers a powerful, alphabetical list of ailments—from minor issues like abdominal cramps to severe conditions like cancer and Parkinson's Disease—and pairs them with affirmations designed to reverse their effects.

As I read through her list, I was mind-blown by how much of it resonated with me. My mom had told me years ago that, as a child, I was plagued with ear infections in both ears. My brother also had ear infections in his right ear and was partially deaf in that ear as well. I decided to look this up on Louise's list of ailments.

Sure enough, it was there: Earache (Otitis), with the probable causes listed as anger, not wanting to hear, too much turmoil, and/or parents arguing (Hay, 1988, p. 49). I mentally checked all of the probable causes off the list. My parents divorced when I was three. Since I was diagnosed at 18 months, I knew there was something there.

The biggest revelation came when I discovered "Deafness" on the list (Hay, 1988, p. 46). I could not believe I had missed it before.

Deafness? I thought. *A thought pattern creates that?*

I felt intrigued. According to Hay, the probable causes of deafness were thought patterns like rejection, stubbornness, isolation, the phrase "Do not bother me," and the question, "What do you not want to hear?" (Hay, 1988, p.

46).

Eager to learn more, I went further down the list and found the word *Incurable*. Louise suggested that "incurable" simply meant it could not be cured externally; true healing required going within, returning the condition to its source (Hay, 1988, p. 66). This meant that despite being deemed incurable by medical standards, deafness indeed had a cure—from within.

I was in shock. Could this really be? Was my dream of hearing naturally actually coming true?

This idea took root in my mind, and I was unable to shake it, no matter how hard I tried.

The seed was firmly planted.

Shortly afterward, I met Mike Connor, my mentor, who created a group called Attracting Grace, inspired by Lynne McTaggart's *The Power of Eight* (2017). In her book, Lynne—a professional journalist and former skeptic—conducted a worldwide experiment in which small groups of people gathered, collectively focusing on a shared intention, such as healing. After experimenting with different group sizes, she discovered that in groups of eight, manifestations occurred almost immediately. She recounted many healings, such as cancer regression, emotional and psychological healing, rapid recovery from severe injuries, and even recovery from paralysis. Mike courageously created Attracting Grace to follow in Lynne's footsteps, and it is thriving today.

When invited to join Mike's group, I eagerly jumped in, intent on healing my hearing. I had heard stories of other self-healings—blind people regaining sight, and paralyzed individuals walking again. Why could I not self-heal my deafness? Just because it was unheard of did not mean it was impossible. The possibility of hearing naturally consumed my thoughts.

This was when everything started to change. Through Mike and his work, I discovered consciousness. I formed a new desire: to raise my level of consciousness. Raising your consciousness means increasing the love you hold. Love heals, while fear destroys. When you elevate your consciousness, your thoughts change, which shifts your inner world—and your outer world. This is where manifestation happens.

A year after meeting Mike and joining Attracting Grace, I went for a routine hearing test. When my audiologist saw the results, she said, "We are going to throw away the previous test because this one is more accurate."

To clarify, Starkey—a renowned facility known for its quality custom hearing aids—had conducted the previous test.

I was silently panicking. With only 2% hearing, I certainly could not afford to lose any more. Concerned, I asked, "Did I lose more hearing?"

"No, not at all," she replied. "This test shows you have more hearing, so the previous one must have been wrong."

Holy cow. I thought. *Is this really happening?*

I knew the Starkey test was more than right. It had been consistent with every other test I had for over 30 years. My hearing had always been the same—until now. This was no mistake. The timing was impeccable, right after I discovered Louise Hay's work and joined Mike's group.

Right then, I knew I was experiencing my first major miracle: I had begun to reverse my hearing loss.

In the days that followed, my hearing steadily improved. I no longer needed captions, nor did I need transcriptions on Zoom calls with clients. Although I was skilled at reading lips, I had always struggled with digital technology. Then one day, while my husband was playing an audiobook in the car, I understood every word. This was a milestone because, before, listening to the radio was like hearing a foreign language—I could not understand a thing without a transcript. But now, I was comprehending it.

One of my favorite moments came shortly after. I heard something without my hearing aids that I had never heard before. I was so excited—it felt like I was a baby hearing for the first time.

This might make you laugh. I was lying in bed one night, trying to sleep, when I heard a strange vibrating noise. At first, I ignored it, but it kept disturbing me.

I thought, *What is that noise? Ugh, I am trying to sleep!*

Wait a minute.

It hit me—I did not have my hearing aids in.

Suddenly, my annoyance turned to excitement. *What is that noise?* I wondered. I was actually hearing something *without* my hearing aids! Then, I realized...

It was my husband snoring.

After 20 years of sleeping beside him, I never knew he snored—until now.

While most people might find snoring annoying, I cherished it. I was so grateful to hear it, and it even helped me sleep peacefully.

After about a year and a half, muscle testing results showed that my hearing had improved by about 20%. My quality of life improved drastically. Where I once needed help or accessibility, I now needed none. My dream was finally coming true.

If I can achieve an impossible dream like that, imagine what you could do!

Emotional Frequency Scale

Enlightenment	700+
Peace	600
Joy	540
Love	500
Reason	400
Acceptance	330
Willingness	310
Neutrality	230
Courage	200
Pride	175
Anger	150
Desire	125
Fear	100
Grief	75
Apathy	50
Guilt	30
Shame	20

Appendix I: The Emotional Scale

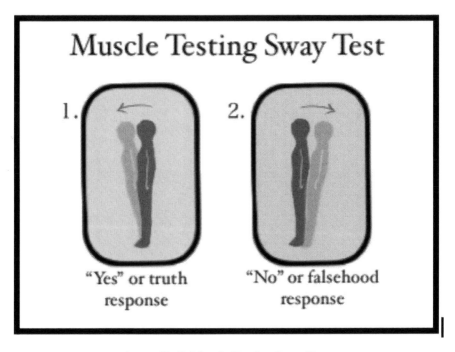

Appendix II: Muscle Testing Sway Test

Your body leans forward with a "yes" response and backward with a "no" response. If the body moves side to side, it means it is a neutral response.

4

A Consciousness Experiment

"Awareness is the greatest agent for change."
— Eckhart Tolle, spiritual teacher and NY Times Best-Selling Author

We are all on a lifelong journey. It is a search for who we are and why we are here. It is a journey that expands our consciousness. In this chapter, we will explore some journaling prompts that guide you through a consciousness experiment. These prompts focus on self-observation, awareness, and exploring how thoughts and beliefs shape reality.

Using reflective and journaling prompts is a powerful way to enhance our level of consciousness. By asking ourselves specific questions, we can direct our focus, shape our thinking, and ultimately elevate our position on the consciousness ladder.

As Eckhart Tolle has said, "Awareness is the greatest agent for change." Without awareness, we simply continue our same life experiences in an infinite number of different ways, albeit with the same emotions. If you face challenging situations and react with negative emotions without understanding why, similar experiences will keep occurring to trigger those same emotions until you learn to see things from a new perspective. Negative emotions could be shame, guilt, grief, anger, or fear, which are all variations of pain.

A *Course in Miracles*, by Helen Schuman teaches us that "Pain thresholds can be high, but they are not limitless. Eventually everyone begins to recognize, however dimly, that there must be a better way" (p. 38). Any negative emotion is the same as pain, and the longer held or repeated, the quicker it manifests into physical pain, illness, or dis-ease in the body.

Have you ever had the experience or wondered why a doctor is unable to give a diagnosis or a reason for great physical pain or illness? The pain is there. Why would no one be able to find it? Surely the person feeling the pain is telling the truth, so why are they the only ones who see it?

There are many cases where people have had many tests done and have gone to many specialists, only to be told there is nothing wrong—yet the physical pain, illness, or dis-ease says otherwise. It is at this point that the body is screaming for awareness. When there is no diagnosis for existing pain, illness, or dis-ease, there is nothing wrong physically, it is all mental. The patterns in the mind have become so toxic that the body is responding in the only way it knows how. Remember this important fact: an emotion is a physical manifestation of the body's reaction to the mind.

When you realize toxic patterns in the mind and intend to shift from fear to love, the body can respond and heal, which ultimately eases the pain. It is quite simple—Love heals. Fear hurts.

The ultimate goal of life is love. Our journey and purpose in life is to make our way back to love, and we do this by first realizing what is going on inside our minds. Expanding our awareness involves becoming more mindful of both our immediate environment and our spiritual role.

When it comes to self-discovery, finding time for reflection can be challenging, especially if you have created a busy life. However, there is a solution—one I have used for several years with incredible effectiveness. As discussed in the previous chapter, muscle testing is a quick and powerful way to bring things into conscious awareness without spending countless hours meditating or waiting for life experiences to reveal insights. Moreover, it has the potential to drastically reduce the amount of pain you may be unconsciously creating by allowing you to make higher choices.

Try the following prompts in quiet contemplation or by writing your thoughts in the space provided or in a personal journal.

In the last section, I have provided a short list of example statements you may calibrate using muscle testing. Record the answers you receive (yes or no) then take a moment to reflect on each one. Allow the thoughts to come without judgment and record any insights you receive.

If you need to review how to do muscle testing, take moment and revisit the Sway Test method in chapter 3.

Journal Prompts to Elevate Your Consciousness

1. Set a timer for five minutes. Allow your awareness to roam without judgment. Remember, the goal is not to control or judge what comes up, but simply to observe with curiosity.

As you sit comfortably, notice where your attention drifts, along with any physical or sensory perceptions that come up. Instead of trying to eliminate distractions, treat this as a guided exploration of what arises naturally. Take the time to journal the following:

- Where does your mind go?
- What sounds and sensations do you experience?
- How do these sensations transition from one to another?

Embrace this journey with complete openness, improving your awareness of everything that is truly present in the moment.

Write your thoughts.

_____
_____
_____
_____
_____
_____

_____

_____

_____

_____

_____

_____

_____

_____

_____

_____

_____

_____

_____

_____

_____

_____

_____

_____

_____

2. Most people do not realize that a negative reaction often means they are holding onto a perspective from the past. Since the past no longer exists, every present experience is fresh—a chance to respond differently and create new outcomes.

When we hold on to the past, we end up reliving it repeatedly in the present moment. For example, anxiety arises from thinking too many thoughts about the future, based on a history of experiences. It is driven by fear of what *could happen,* rooted in judgments and experiences we heard, saw, or felt in the past. On the other hand, depression comes from an over-focus on the past, fueled by regret and thoughts of *what could have been.*

By failing to let go of the past, we prevent ourselves from being present, which blocks us from being truly conscious and accessing higher levels of thought.

Visual Exercise

Take a moment to think of a problem, issue, or challenge you are facing right now.

1. Close your eyes and imagine yourself as a being with no past. You simply imagine—there is no need to worry if this feels unrealistic.
2. Pretend you are an actor with a brand-new role. You are handed a manuscript with everything happening at this moment, but there is no mention of the past or how you got here. Set aside any judgments, thoughts, or reasoning that say, "This is not possible."
3. Spend a few minutes imagining yourself with no past. Set a timer if you would like to stay focused. Breathe deeply and allow yourself to feel what it is like to be present, with no history attached to who you are.
4. After a few minutes, bring the problem or issue you thought of before back to mind. What is different? Do you find you have a difficult time remembering or feeling connected to that challenge?

Reflection

The present moment is all we have. The past no longer exists. By momentarily imagining yourself as a being with no past, you enter a state of innocence, allowing your mind to be more open and receptive.

Now, sit with this idea for a few minutes and explore how experiencing life in the present moment affects you. Reflect on these questions:

- How does it feel to view your life without any prior assumptions or judgments?
- How might this shift in perspective positively impact your current state of being?
- Are there other areas of your life where this perspective could be useful?
- In what ways could this outlook bring more ease and clarity to your life?

Take your time journaling on these reflections and allow yourself to explore the possibilities of living more fully in the present.

3. In the previous exercise, you explored what it might feel like to exist in the present moment without a past, experiencing life with fresh eyes. Now, let's dive deeper into this concept of "beginner's mind" and explore how suspending past judgments and assumptions can change your perception. When you change your perception, you change your perspective, and when you change your perspective, you raise your consciousness. It really is that simple!

When we interact with the world, we often bring a collection of assumptions, judgments, and beliefs shaped by our past experiences. These can color the way we view ourselves, others, and our potential. But what if, just for a moment, we could approach each situation as if we were encountering it for the first time?

Take some time to reflect on these questions and consider how you can continue practicing a beginner's mind in your daily life. Allow yourself to be curious, open, and free from the weight of past judgments as you explore each new moment.

1. **Choose a Recent Experience:** Think about something that recently bothered you, challenged you, or caused you stress. It could be a conversation, a project, or even a moment of self-doubt.
2. **Rewrite the Experience with a Beginner's Mind:** Now, imagine yourself as a newcomer to this experience, with no prior assumptions or judgments about it. Close your eyes and take a few deep breaths, clearing your mind.

- Approach this experience as if you are witnessing it for the first time, with no history or attachment to what it "should" mean or how it "should" feel. For example, you could imagine that you are a traveler from another world, observing this situation with fresh eyes. What do you notice when you let go of all past impressions?

Write your thoughts on the next page.

49

_____

_____

_____

_____

_____

_____

_____

_____

_____

_____

_____

_____

_____

_____

_____

_____

_____

_____

_____

_____

_____

_____

_____

_____

_____

Reflect on Your Observations: Spend a few minutes journaling about what you noticed during this exercise. Consider the following questions:

- How did your view of the situation change when you removed your past assumptions?

- Did new insights or feelings emerge?
- How did this fresh perspective shift your understanding of the situation?

Write your thoughts.

_____

_____

_____

_____

_____

_____

_____

_____

_____

_____

_____

_____

_____

_____

_____

_____

_____

_____

_____

_____

_____

_____

_____

_____

_____

Further Reflection

Now, think about how adopting a beginner's mind could impact other areas of your life:

- How might approaching people, situations, or yourself with a fresh perspective improve your interactions and experiences?
- What assumptions do you frequently carry about yourself or others, and how do they influence your behavior?
- How could letting go of these judgments bring more freedom, openness, and curiosity into your life?

_____
_____
_____
_____
_____
_____
_____
_____
_____
_____
_____
_____
_____
_____
_____
_____
_____
_____
_____
_____

5

The Unconscious Mind—The Missing Piece

"Until you make the unconscious conscious, it will direct your life,
and you will call it FATE."
— *Carl Jung, Swiss Psychiatrist and Psychoanalyst.*

The Unconscious is the part of the mind that is based on feelings and is an automatic processing center. Also known as the body, it carries its actions out and requires no thinking. For example, do you think about brushing your teeth, drinking a glass of water, riding a bike, or driving a car? Most likely not. After many repetitions, your body knows and performs these actions automatically.

This part of you is very trainable, and it learns and is, maybe, the key to your mind's power. We *teach* the unconscious by what we choose to do repeatedly until it becomes second nature. Take riding a bike, for example. When you first learned how to ride a bike, it was challenging and you likely fell many times. Perhaps you even experienced bruises. However, this did not make you stop, did it? You continued to practice until you got it, and then off you went, riding freely into the wind.

Now, we only get to do those things that our unconscious believes are safe for us to attempt. Why? Because its only job is to keep the body alive. In the earlier example, look back to the time you were riding your bike and focus on how you felt before getting on.

You most likely felt a mixture of uncomfortable emotions, such as anxiety, fear, nervousness, and self-doubt. If you were learning with someone else, you may have also felt a sense of vulnerability and fear of being embarrassed or failing. You may have felt many sensations in your body as a result, such as your heart racing, palms sweating, or a tightness in your chest.

All of this is normal, but why does that happen?

Because you have not survived it yet. It is all a direct result of your unconscious mind trying to stop you because it sees that it is something *new* and, therefore, sees it as a threat. It believes you will die. If this part of you feels unsafe, it will throw up all sorts of feelings such as shame, fear, guilt, frustration, or overwhelm.

Can you remember when you started anything else that was new? How did you feel when you first thought about it, before you decided and took the first action? These emotions and feelings are all created by the unconscious mind. Then, once you take the action and you do not die, the unconscious adds it to its repertoire of approved experiences and helps you achieve it instead of hindering you. It is trainable and is, perhaps, the key to the mind's power.

The Power of the Unconscious in Shaping Reality

The unconscious mind, which is the part of us that allows what we create, has its roots in fear. When you get an idea from the heart, it goes through the unconscious mind first, which then accepts or denies it based on survivability.

In many of his works, Carl Jung discussed how the unconscious mind influences our psyche and how it processes and filters ideas before they reach our conscious awareness. As such, our conscious thoughts are deeply connected to the unconscious. (*Carl Jung on the Unconscious and Dreams*, 2015).

Since the only job of the unconscious mind is to keep us safe, it will refuse anything new as it sees it as a threat. It will do everything in its power to stop you from moving forward with the experience until you do. Once you go through something and come out the other side, your unconscious mind recognizes it and wants to have more of that experience. It will help you do it long enough until it becomes automatic and second nature. It becomes your ally, instead of your enemy, until you decide to create or do something else that is new. Then, the process starts all over again.

From birth to 4 or 7 years of age, everything we survive is "coded up" as survivable, which makes the unconscious want more of it. It affects the thoughts we receive, as well as influencing our choices. Often, we are unaware of the unconscious intent and discover we keep creating the same experiences.

This is why anyone would repeat abusive relationships, run out of money, or chronically get sick. It is because we have survived them all and the unconscious wants more of it until we are courageous enough to choose differently.

If you grew up with a distant father, for example, you will later be distant from the masculine, because this is what you survived. Or, if you grew up from trauma, shame, or scarcity, you will repeat those experiences *because you survived them.* If you grew up in a system where everyone worked hard for money, then it will be the same for you as an adult, until you decide to change it.

Why?

Because you survived it.

Get the picture? Anything opposite to what we have experienced is dangerous to the unconscious. This creates a lifelong battle between the one part of us that wishes to create effortlessly and get everything it wants. It wants everything in life to be grand and new and exciting.

Then, we have this *other* part of us that is unconscious (and invisible) to us that only wants to do what it has already survived, *regardless of how painful or traumatic it is!* It is the ultimate cosmic joke played on humanity to give us this awakened consciousness with an unconsciousness that says "I am not changing under any circumstances." Then we get to say to ourselves that we need to get rid of procrastination, poor money habits, or other fears and negative beliefs, without actually changing any of it.

Until we get courageous, actually do it, and survive.

The Contradiction Trap

All the time, we contradict ourselves. We want more money but fail to do what is necessary to get it, or we fail to recognize and seize the opportunities as they arise. Or, we want a loving relationship but make excuses and find everything wrong with a person on the first date. Perhaps we want happiness, but complain about why we do not have it. The unconscious is accepting all of it, which is what creates a stuck experience. Nothing will ever manifest, except more of what we do not want.

Most of our contradictions are from a concern of failing, or from a focus on the process instead of the end result. The problems become part of the suggestion to the unconscious, which keeps you stuck.

"I want it, but..."

This is the silent killer.

The unconscious mind accepts everything as truth because it processes information literally, without questioning or analyzing it. It will continue to manifest whatever it concludes. This is why you see some people take so many courses and they still do not have the money they desire or the answers they seek.

We get all our beliefs and suggestions from our upbringing and the world around us. If you have the belief that you must work hard for money, this means your parents or caregivers, teachers, friends, and acquaintances all contributed to it, and we believe we need to do it that way too. It was an unconscious suggestion that we accepted and it said yes to.

Here is an example:

Joe wishes to buy a car. He has decided that this will enhance his life, and goes out to look for one. The following is his thought process:

Joe: *I want a car*

Unconscious: *OK, let's go get a car*

Joe: *How will I get a car? It is hard to finance a car and interest rates are high.*

Unconscious: *Yes to both.*

Joe: *And I should consider if I want Gas or EV. I will have to do the research.*

Unconscious: *You bet.*

Joe: *And then there are taxes to consider. And insurance. That can be expensive.*

Unconscious: *Absolutely, you are right*

Joe: *I do not think I have enough money to get a car.*

Unconscious: *I guess not.*

Joe's unconscious has created a worldview that says it is hard and expensive to buy a car. But, is this really true?

There are plenty of people that find great deals on cars, save on taxes, and even save on insurance. But, for Joe, he will never find it. Why? Because he/his unconscious set it up that way.

What we must do is give the unconscious *clear, strong suggestions*, and then let the unconscious create the rest. You do this by keeping your focus on the end result of what you wish to create—not the unconscious *noise.* The unconscious will create what you focus on.

Here is how it would work:

Joe: *I want a car.*

Unconscious: *OK, let's get a car*

Joe: *I would love to find a car that is economical with all the technological bells and whistles.*

Unconscious: *Let's do it*

Joe: *I would love for it to be within my budget of $400 a month or less, with low interest rates, and with no money down.*

Unconscious: *Ok*

Joe: *And I want it to be new, or softly used*

Unconscious: *Yep*

Joe: *I want affordable insurance, and I would love to find a way to save on the* *taxes*

Unconscious: *Alright, you got it*

Now, Joe simply lets the thoughts go and lets his unconscious do the work. Within a few days, he gets a call from an old friend of his who is looking to sell his car to get out of debt. He communicates to Joe that the car possesses very low mileage, brand-new tires, navigation, and an upgraded sound system. It is a hybrid vehicle and gets close to 35-40 miles to the gallon. He will let it go for what he currently owes the bank, as he just needs to get rid of it.

Joe calls his credit union and applies for a loan. Because of his excellent history with the bank, the bank agrees to pay off his friend's car with no money down and gives Joe a very low interest rate, which brings his monthly payment well below his budget. Because the car is a hybrid, he can save on his taxes.

Joe gets his car and lives happily ever after.

The unconscious always finds a way. This is what it means to surrender. You decide what you want, make it clear, and let it go. The unconscious will get it to you. If you are looking for a relationship, career, or any other subject, replace the car example above with what it is you wish to create, and remember, the unconscious follows all of your suggestions.

Remember, make it clear!

6

Reflecting and Exploring Unconscious Patterns

*"Your body knows exactly what to do. It heals itself, if you allow it to,
but it requires a conscious awareness of that which you are blocking."*
— *Nicole Reina*

As you learned in the previous chapter, unconscious patterns affect and control everything that happens in our lives. Regardless of how many affirmations you do, mantras you chant, or meditations you complete, nothing will ever override your unconscious patterning until you choose to make it conscious.

You make anything conscious by bringing awareness to it. Once you become aware, it becomes a light shining in the dark, offering healing and a chance to truly change your life.

When I discovered that anger was the root cause of my profound hearing loss, it created an awareness of how I hear. I discovered that as I listened to people talk, the thoughts in my mind ranged from criticism to frustration and everything in between. Before I became aware, because of my past trauma, perceived injustices, and constant conditioning to fend on my own, I took everything personally, which affected the way I listened. I discovered I never listened with an impartial ear, even when I thought I did. I held an unconscious pattern where I constantly judged everything I heard instead of simply listening without judgment.

When I became aware of this pattern, it became so clear to me how I had created many traumatic moments and blamed others instead of taking time to reflect and accept responsibility. So many of my experiences simply came from misunderstanding and flawed perceptions. When I courageously accepted this and actively worked to improve my listening skills, my hearing loss reversed. I changed my perception of what I heard, which raised my consciousness. My body let go of the pattern of creating deafness and created hearing instead.

Journaling Prompts

1. *Uncovering Unconscious Patterns*

Think of a pattern in your life that keeps repeating, whether it is a relationship dynamic, a habit, or a financial situation. Reflect on the following questions:

- What beliefs, memories, or past experiences might influence this pattern?
- How do these patterns make you feel? Do they feel familiar, even if they are not necessarily positive?
- If you were to imagine a different outcome, how would you respond? Would you feel safe or uncomfortable with this new outcome? Why?

Spend some time exploring the connection between your unconscious mind and these patterns. How might acknowledging these influences help you consciously reshape them?

Write your thoughts.

_____

_____

_____

2. *Challenging the Comfort Zone*

Resistance is the mechanism by which we fail to do what we choose. It shows up in a variety of ways, such as procrastination, excuses, distractions, etc. Laziness does not exist. This is a judgment placed on resisting change, and is actually an extreme form of procrastination, which is an unconscious pattern put in place to keep you the same. It is **not** you!

Any action (or no action) except the next right action to bring you closer to the goal is an action to keep you the same. Resistance is the fear created by the unconscious to ensure we stay the same—so we can survive. We will most likely never choose to do anything that can kill us, yet the unconscious believes that doing *anything new* means you (and it) will die. It only changes its mind after you have done it and survived. This is what the phrase "face your fears" really means. Once you have done this, it is no longer a threat to the unconscious.

Think of something you have been wanting to do or change but are resisting. This could be a new move, a new relationship, a health goal, a financial goal, a career move, or even a creative project.

- List any fears, doubts, or beliefs that arise when you consider taking this action. How does your body respond—are there any physical sensations tied to these thoughts?
- Reflect on how your unconscious mind might perceive this action as a threat, even if it could ultimately lead to positive growth. Where does this fear come from?
- Now, imagine that you have taken the right action, and you have come out on the other side successfully. How does it feel? What might it take to convince your unconscious that this action is safe and worth pursuing?

On the next page, journal any insights or shifts in perception that come up as you visualize this future success.

3. *Rewriting Your Unconscious Script*

Choose one belief about yourself or your life that you recognize may be holding you back. This could be a belief like "I am not good enough," "I am not worthy of money or love," "I have to work hard to succeed," "I do not have enough education," "I do not have a degree," "I always fail in relationships," "I am sick or ill or unhealthy," "Everyone rejects me," or even "I am sick and tired of being sick and tired!"

You must know this to be true: any belief you hold that prevents you from getting what you want is a false belief. We can have anything, be anything, and do anything we want. There are no limits, nor is anyone limiting **you** except yourself. There are no rules, except the rules you give yourself.

If I chose to believe that healing my deafness was as impossible as society and medicine say, then I would not be experiencing the miracles I am today.

Now, let's examine your false beliefs and bring them to light. Take some time to reflect and journal your thoughts on the following:

- Where do you think this belief originated? Try to connect it to past experiences or influences.
- Consider how this belief shapes your behavior today. How does it limit your choices or hold you back from trying new things?
- Rewrite this belief as an empowering statement. For example, change "I have to work hard to succeed" to "I attract success by following my passion and intuition." Reflect on how this new belief feels and visualize your unconscious mind accepting it as truth.

Spend a few minutes each day reinforcing this new belief, and observe any changes in your thoughts, actions, or feelings.

Write your thoughts.

_____

_____

_____

7

Creating Your Desire

"Within you, is the divine capacity to manifest and attract all that you desire. "
—*Dr. Wayne Dyer, renowned Self-Help Author and Motivational Speaker*

A s I mentioned earlier in this book, emotions drive manifestation. In the example of Joe in the previous chapter, when Joe was thinking about buying a car, can you guess what his emotional state was by looking at his thoughts?

In the first example, Joe was pessimistic, and worried about money. If we were to calibrate the example using Dr. Hawkins' method with the emotional frequency scale, it would calibrate in grief, because he wants a car but thinks he cannot afford it. Therefore, because of the principle of the law of attraction, the actual experiences he attracts cannot bring him anything but more grief. He will probably only see cars that are out of his price range, and if he finds a car in his price range, the taxes will be high or the insurance will be expensive. Either way, Joe's experience would be the end result of not affording the car.

In the second example, we would find that the level of consciousness of Joe's thought process calibrates in the emotion of courage, which means the experiences he attracts will likely be favorable. Remember, according to the scale of emotions, fear is rooted in anything below 200, and love is rooted in anything above 200. Since courage falls above 200, the experiences that are attracted will tilt in favor of what Joe wants. Since he surrendered to the unconscious and did not try to control the outcome of the experience, his unconscious could bring him a very favorable result.

If Joe had known about muscle testing, he could have used it to evaluate the energy of his thoughts in the first example and easily shifted them to more positive, higher-energy thoughts, as in the second example. To do this, he would write his thoughts and then make statements like "This thought serves me" (Y/N) or "This thought calibrates over 200 on a scale of 1-1000 on Dr. Hawkins' emotional frequency scale" (Y/N). Now, try it for yourself! Go through Joe's thoughts in the first example, and use your preferred method of muscle testing to get your answer.

To shift your thoughts, simply intend to find a higher thought and see what comes up. Write it down, then calibrate the new thought by using your chosen muscle testing method. Continue this process until you land on a thought that is over 200. Then, choose it!

This is where the power of calibration, the process of muscle testing, comes in—you do not need to know your exact emotional state to figure out where you calibrate energetically. This comes in handy for those of us (like me) who are numb to emotions. By calibrating where we are consciously, or our thought process, we can consciously create favorable outcomes, instead of leaving it all to our unconscious.

Teaching the Unconscious: The Power of Effective Visualization

To manifest your desires, it is crucial to focus entirely on the end result. The unconscious mind responds to what you choose to think about, but it only acts on what you consciously select. Since the unconscious mind's primary goal is to keep you safe, it may create emotions and thoughts that lead you away from your desire, especially if you have never experienced it before. If you follow these unconscious prompts, your original desire becomes irrelevant because you are allowing the unconscious to steer you away from your goal. Instead, you need to consciously direct your mind by visualizing the outcome you desire and staying focused on achieving that result.

The only way to get the unconscious to give you what you want without resistance is to teach it.

Here is a fact: The unconscious does not know the difference between what is imagined and what is real. Remember, the Now is all we have, and you must teach your unconscious that you already have what you want right now, so it believes you have survived it. It does not matter if you can see it, smell it, taste it, or touch it in your current reality. The only thing that matters is that you imagine it as if you had it right now.

You must *visualize* it into life with emotion, repeatedly, until the unconscious becomes comfortable and believes it can survive the experience. This is the hack.

The past is over, and the future has yet to be created. You use your imagination to go into the future and imagine yourself having your desires right in this very moment. Hold this vision long enough to feel it, then even longer to experience the emotion of it.

Emotion is key.

You teach your unconscious through emotions. Right now, you can have it all. Everything starts in the imagination first, then it becomes visible as a physical manifestation. Everything started as a thought, an idea, then it was created. Think about the lightbulb. Edison had to imagine it first, then he brought it to life.

There is a formula to this. It is:

Thought+Feeling+Emotion = Manifestation of desire

You must visualize the *end result* of your desire as if it is already done, and experience the *emotion* you would feel if you had it right now. It is time to do

70

some practice.

Visualization Exercise to Get Into the End Result

Abraham-Hicks has said, "If you can visualize it, if you are dreaming it, it is already on the way." (Dimas 20).

I would love for you to choose one thing you would love to create. Just one, as we can only do one thing at a time. It is like when you are at a restaurant and ordering from the menu. You order one thing at a time, you do not order the entire menu at once.

So, think about what you would love to create. Perhaps you would like a loving relationship, a healthy marriage, an exciting career, more money than you could spend, etc. Or, it could be a non-physical desire, such as peace, happiness, prosperity, abundance, or even tranquility. The world is your oyster!

This is a closed eye exercise. Once you have chosen the desire you wish to create, read through the exercise, close your eyes and imagine the experience, ensuring to hold the vision long enough to generate emotion.

An emotion could be tears of happiness and gratitude streaming down your cheeks, laughter, or perhaps the sensation of joy in your chest. Whatever emotion it is for you, the key is to express it. This is what will teach the unconscious that the experience is real, and survivable.

This is not a one and done exercise. You must continue this practice until the unconscious stops resisting it. When you think about your desire and feel resistance, it means your unconscious still does not believe it is safe.

This is where many people fail. When you visualize the end result of how you want it to be, you must hold the vision until you express emotion, surrender the experience to the unconscious (meaning do not think about it—just be grateful that it is done), and then do the process again the next day, until you no longer feel resistance to your desire. You must stay consistent and mindful. In the below exercise, be sure to pause for a few seconds or more after each question to allow for your mind to conjure up ideas. This is meant to be a slow process, but should not take more than 15 minutes.

Ready? Let's practice!

Visualization Exercise

With your eyes closed, in your mind's eye, step into the end result of whatever your choice is.

.

In your mind, step into the end result of.........blank.

.

And as you choose it, please pick a time in the future where you are actually living this experience.

.

Think about what it would look like, in as much detail as possible.
Are you outside or inside?
Who are you with?
What are you doing?
What smells are there? Any visual objects? What about sound? What does it sound like?
You already have your chosen desire. What thoughts are you thinking?

.

Now...Focus on how you feel. How does it feel?
How does it feel to live... the end result of... your choice?

.

What do you notice about it?
Is there anything that you might say to yourself like...... this is the fullest experience I have ever imagined?

.

Again, go into the end result.
Find a time when you are living it.
See it.
With your own eyes.
Feel it with your whole body.

.

What...does it feel like?
Really focus on the feeling...hold the feeling.
What emotions are bubbling up?
Notice where in your body you feel it. Where do you feel it the most?
Get to the emotion...are you grateful? Happy? Elated? How does it feel?
Express it.

.

Now...Truly choose the experience.
Say to yourself or out loud:
I choose to experience this end result of ...

.

I choose to experience this end result of...

.

Really choose it with all of your heart and soul, and decide how it is.

.

I choose to experience this end result of...
Decide how you want it to be.

.

And when you are ready, come on back.
And think to yourself...

.

How do I feel?

How did it feel to be in that experience, which is the end result of your choice that you have not been able to accept as of this time?

You have now become a magnet for your desire. You must HOLD this energy no matter what comes your way....and you do this....by being grateful.

Because Gratitude means...it is done.

8

Aligning Desire: Muscle Testing for Clarity

"The intuitive mind is a sacred gift and the rational mind is a faithful servant. We have created a society that honors the servant and has forgotten the gift." – Albert Einstein

As you have learned, muscle testing offers a practical tool for tapping into the body's wisdom, bringing hidden beliefs, emotions, or energetic blocks into awareness. By making simple statements and observing the body's physical response, we can bypass the mind's chatter and access deeper truths. Additionally, by using muscle testing, we are able to discern choices that move us toward our desires and away from pain.

When I first started using muscle testing, I was blown away by the effectiveness of this tool and loved the fact that I no longer had to rely on my thoughts to get answers. As an avid overthinker, I struggled for a long time with anxiety. Because I lacked the skillset needed to truly make good decisions, I found myself making more mistakes than I needed to and experienced painful situations that I had unconsciously created, thinking I was doing the opposite.

I often made decisions based on my gut instinct (which is rooted in fear). What many people fail to realize is that your gut instinct is a primal response, driven by the need to survive and past experiences. It originates from the aspect of you that needs to protect and control, reacting to perceived threats.

On the other hand, intuition is a calm, inner knowing that transcends the ego, that part of you that is focused on survival. It comes from a deeper connection to your higher self, guiding you toward alignment with your true purpose, without imposed fear or limitations.

In order to manifest your desires, you must be in alignment with them. Muscle testing offers a way to navigate your current alignment and find the awareness needed to raise your energy so that you are vibrating at the level needed to attract what you want. By making the right statements and adjusting your choices, you allow yourself to receive the highest good that is intended for all of us.

Muscle testing acts as a bridge to access your intuition by bypassing the analytical mind and the ego. It taps into the body's natural intelligence, allowing you to connect with your inner knowing. Through subtle physical responses, muscle testing reveals what your intuition already understands, offering a tangible way to align with deeper truths and gain clarity on decisions or beliefs.

The Importance of Water

As you have been reading this book, your consciousness has likely risen and your energy has begun to shift. Before we dive into the activity, allow me to share with you the importance of drinking water. As you learned in Chapter 3, in order for muscle testing to be effective and accurate, your body must be well-hydrated. Here is why:

1. **Increased Mental Activity:** Consciousness work, like deep meditation, visualization, or energy-based practices, increases brain activity. Since the brain (and your body) is 75% water, staying hydrated supports optimal cognitive function and focus.
2. **Energetic Shifts:** Consciousness work involves subtle energy shifts. Water is a natural conductor of energy, which helps the body process and integrate these shifts more smoothly. Hydration aids in balancing and grounding this energetic flow.
3. **Detoxification:** As you raise your awareness and work through emotional

or energetic blocks, the mind and body may trigger a detox process. It is important to understand that the body stores emotions, and when negative emotions are released, the body may initiate a detoxification process to process them. This can manifest in various ways, such as sudden tears, unexplained pain, muscle twitches, and more. Drinking plenty of water helps flush out the toxins released during this process, aiding in a smoother emotional and physical cleanse.

4. **Physical Sensitivity:** Consciousness work can heighten your body's sensitivity to subtle changes, which means you may notice signs of dehydration sooner (e.g., fatigue, headaches, or difficulty concentrating). Staying well-hydrated ensures your body remains in balance.

Muscle Testing Activity

Use the following statements to guide your muscle testing practice, uncover insights, and align your energy with your highest intentions. Use the provided statements as a guide to help you get started.

As you prepare to do this activity, take a moment and take three deep breaths, in through the nose and out through the mouth to help you relax and clear your mind. Set the intention that you wish to communicate to your body. Remember, you must be willing to release all attachments and be open to receiving the highest truth.

If you find that you are resisting a certain statement, it means you are attached to the response. For the answer to be effective, you must take a moment to release all attachments by stating *"I intend to release all attachments to this statement and wish to receive pure truth for the highest good of all."*

In the statements below, Circle the Y or N response you get, and use the journaling section below or a personal journal to record your thoughts and insights.

1. **I am fully hydrated (Y/N)**—If you get a no answer, stop and get yourself a glass of water. Remember, you must be fully hydrated for muscle testing to be fully effective.

2. Take an item from your pantry or refrigerator that you eat often, or a supplement you take regularly. Hold it to your chest and state: **This food (or supplement) is beneficial for my body (Y/N)**— If the answer is no, decide if you choose to stop consuming it. Remember, we all have the free will to make our own choices. However, if you continue to use something your body has indicated is not beneficial, be mindful of the potential consequences and take responsibility for your decision.

3. **I am grounded and fully present in this moment (Y/N)**—If no, refer to chapter 5 in the section titled "Become Rooted in the Now".

4. **I am aligned with my highest purpose (Y/N)**—A 'no' response does not mean you are on the wrong path; it is simply an awareness that there is room for realignment or deeper reflection. This is an opportunity to pause and reassess. Ask yourself what areas of your life feel out of sync with your genuine desires or values. What adjustments can you make to move closer to your highest purpose? Trust that this awareness is a gift—it is guiding you toward greater alignment and fulfillment.

5. Think about a decision you need to make, then make the following statement: **This decision (or path) is in my best interest (Y/N)**—If no, decide to either move forward anyway, or ask to be shown other options. Write down what comes to mind, then do the process again until you receive a yes response.

6. **I am open to receiving abundance (Y/N)**—If no, find out where the resistance is. It could be financial, emotional, or spiritual. State the following 'I am resistant to receiving (financial, emotional, spiritual) abundance (Y/N)' and record the response you receive. Take time to reflect on the answers you receive and write them down.

7. Think of a relationship or a person that you spend a lot of time with, and make the following statement: **This relationship (or person) is supportive of my growth and well-being (Y/N)**—If no, reflect on the relationship or person, and think about how you may either reduce the time spent with them or find time to communicate your needs.

8. **My body is free of toxins (Y/N)**—If you get a 'no' response, this does not mean something is wrong. Your body may be signaling the need for

extra care and attention. Consider taking steps to support your body's natural detoxification processes, such as drinking more water, eating whole foods, getting adequate rest, and perhaps exploring practices like gentle exercise, deep breathing, or detoxifying baths. Listen to your body. Trust that by making small, conscious adjustments, you are helping to restore balance and well-being.

9. **I trust my intuition and inner guidance (Y/N)**—If no, it means there is room to strengthen your connection with yourself. Set the intention that you will trust yourself more, take time to quiet your mind, practice self-reflection, and trust that as you tune in more deeply, your inner guidance will become clearer and more reliable.

10. **I am worthy of love and success (Y/N)**—If you get a 'no' response, there may be underlying beliefs blocking your sense of worthiness. Take this as an invitation to explore and release those limiting beliefs, reminding yourself daily that you are deserving of love and success, simply by being who you are.

11. Think of a place that you frequent often and make the statement: **This location (or environment) supports my well-being (Y/N)**

12. **I am ready to release this emotional block of ____(fear, anger, resentment) (Y/N)**—If you get a no response, respect your body and simply move on. It just means that there are aspects of you that are resisting growth. This is OK and perfectly natural. Give yourself some time, practice self-care, and speak to yourself with loving words. In a day or two, revisit this question.

13. As there are a myriad of different healing modalities and tools available today, not all of them align with your body's needs at the time. To discern a healing method you would like to use, make the following statement: **This healing method (or practice) is right for me at this time (Y/N).**

This is just a short list of examples to help you begin your muscle-testing journey. Keep in mind, as tempting as it may be, muscle testing cannot predict the future—so no, it will not help you win the lottery! :)

If you are looking for additional guidance on muscle testing, there are coaches available who can help you navigate the process and create powerful statements to align with your desires. It is important to find a coach (like myself) who is familiar with Dr. Hawkins and his work, so you may pursue the highest path possible.

9

The Power of Nature in Elevating Your Consciousness

"The goal of life is to make your heartbeat match the beat of the universe, to match your nature with Nature."
– *Joseph Campbell, American Mythologist, Writer, and Lecturer*

I used to find nature boring. If given the choice between going to a park or catching a movie, I would always pick the movie. Why? Because I had no idea what to do at the park. To me, the park meant heat, long walks that led to blisters, and nothing to look at but trees, grass, bugs, and the occasional flower. It felt about as exciting as brushing my teeth.

I preferred the adrenaline rush I got from an exciting movie or a roller coaster at an amusement park. Nature was simply a backdrop—something that was just "there." I paid little attention to my surroundings unless they were directly thrust into my experience, like a bouquet of flowers or an unusual animal crossing my path.

Sadly enough, I was not alone. In the book *Dance With the Earth* by Sharla Lee Shults, she states that "Society has shifted us from awe-inspiring nature to spending an average of ninety-three percent (93%) of time indoors (U.S.

EPA, 2001)," (Shults, 2024). Unfortunately, this has not changed since the COVID pandemic.

In my life leading up to the pandemic, the saying "stop and smell the roses" held little meaning for me because it felt like a waste of time. I was always too busy chasing goals, always in motion, believing I could rest once I "got there." One of my favorite sayings was, "I will sleep when I am dead." I was constantly on the go, running at full speed, convinced that any pause meant falling behind.

To keep up with this relentless pace, I turned to caffeine. At first, it was coffee, then espresso, and eventually, energy drinks. I even resorted to pre-workout drinks like Redline Xtreme and Jack3d, which packed the caffeine equivalent of almost four cups of coffee. My addiction lasted for decades.

Happiness, for me, was tied to achieving something, earning praise, or doing something exciting. I believed that if I could reach my goals faster, I would finally be the person I wanted to be. What I failed to realize was that this constant chase was pulling me further from myself.

The Wake-Up Call

I had an unconscious belief that I was not good enough—a belief so toxic that it nearly cost me my life. When I finally woke up to who I really was in 2020, I had strayed so far from my true self that I found myself teetering on the edge of suicide, not once, but several times.

Nature is what saved me.

Most people fail to realize that nature is more than just scenery; it is a profound teacher and healer, offering wisdom and elevation for our consciousness. We often treat nature poorly—destroying forests, littering, and displacing animals. The truth is, if we truly understood the power nature holds, we would treat it, and ourselves, with much more respect.

Nature holds the key to raising our consciousness, bringing us into alignment with our deepest desires, and restoring a sense of peace in a world that often feels chaotic. In many ways, nature is the antidote to our overactive minds.

The Connection Between Nature and Elevating Consciousness

To raise our consciousness and attract more of what we want into our lives, we must become aware of the unconscious patterns that hold us back. This requires disconnecting from the distractions of everyday life so what is buried in our unconscious mind can then rise to the surface. It is like holding a cork underwater—the constant pressure keeps us from seeing clearly. When we become present, the cork floats to the surface, bringing hidden truths with it.

Meditation is a powerful tool for this, but the environment matters. Nature, with its inherent stillness, amplifies the benefits of meditation. Even a short walk in nature can have profound effects, bringing clarity and healing on both physical and energetic levels.

Studies have shown that when we spend time in nature, stress is lowered and our immune system is boosted. In fact, being in nature can actually help combat cancer cells. Certain trees, such as pines, firs, cedars and cypresses, release phytoncides. These are chemicals that stimulate the body's production of natural killer cells, which combat cancer cells.

Additionally, simply being in a natural setting boosts dopamine and endorphins, which are emotional states that elevate consciousness.

Nature teaches us to be present and accept life as it unfolds. Just as a flower endures harsh weather and pests before it blooms, we too must embrace life's challenges with grace. Nature does not resist—it flows. Aligning with the energetic frequency of what we wish to create begins with acceptance.

Nature as a Healer

When I finally woke up to my unconscious patterns, I found that even the quiet of my home was insufficient to heal the mental illnesses I had developed over years of living in overdrive. It was not until I spent time in nature that my symptoms truly began to subside. Nature's calming presence helped me clear my mind, and I started to see the importance of advocating for its preservation.

We need nature as much as it needs us. Think of the symbiotic relationship we share with trees: we exhale carbon dioxide, which they need, and they provide the oxygen we need in return. This balance reflects the harmony we should strive for in our own lives.

Research shows that spending time in nature reduces stress, improves mental clarity, and lowers blood pressure. These are the physical benefits. On an energetic level, nature helps clear emotional blockages and raise our frequency, which is essential for attracting more of what we desire in life. As we let go of stress and embrace presence, we naturally elevate our consciousness and begin to experience life from a place of peace and clarity.

Nature's Role in Manifestation

To manifest your desires, you must align your energetic vibration with what you want to create. You cannot plant seeds of scarcity and expect to reap abundance. If you seek love, you must first love yourself. Remember, as the Law of Attraction states, like attracts like. Your beliefs must match the reality you want to experience. You must *be* it to *see* it. To attract love, you must *be* love. To attract money, you must *be* abundant and prosperous.

Nature offers a perfect example of alignment and non-resistance. Just as a tree grows without effort and a river flows without struggle, you too can manifest your desires with ease when you align your energy. Like changing a station on the radio, the key is to change the frequency of your thoughts—not the thoughts themselves. This shift in consciousness allows you to access higher thoughts and better ideas, with non-resistance.

In nature, everything has a season: a time for growth, a time for harvest, a time for rest. When we embrace this cyclical process in our own lives, we manifest more effortlessly. Impatience only comes from focusing on the absence of what we desire. The next time you feel stuck or impatient, spend time in nature to recalibrate and reconnect with the flow of life.

A Simple Exercise for Mindfulness

In order to be present, mindfulness is required, which is a skill that takes practice to master. Being mindful means you are actively engaging with your surroundings through all of your senses. It means you are present. We have likely had decades of practice in doing the opposite (i.e. overthinking), so it will take time and effort to disconnect from the mind and achieve consistent presence. Nature offers a fun and easy environment to assist in enhancing your connection to nature and elevating your consciousness.

In her book *Dance With the Earth*, Sharla Lee Shults (2024) offers beautiful insight and inspiration that helps you to tap into the wonderful world of nature. Here is a simple exercise from her book that offers a great way to connect and practice mindfulness:

The Sensory Awareness Exercise

1. **Find a Quiet Outdoor Space:** Go outside and find a natural spot where you feel calm and relaxed. It can be a garden, park, forest, or even your backyard.
2. **Close Your Eyes and Breathe:** Begin by taking deep breaths. Inhale through your nose, and exhale slowly. Focus on the sensation of the air entering and leaving your
3. lungs. Let the stresses of the day fall away.
4. **Engage Your Senses One by One:**

- **Sight:** Open your eyes and observe the details around you. Move beyond just seeing—really focus on observing. Notice the texture of leaves, the patterns of sunlight on the ground, the movement of birds or insects.
- **Smell:** Breathe in the fragrances around you. Perhaps there is the scent of grass, flowers, or even the earthy smell of the soil.
- **Sound:** Listen carefully to the sounds of nature. Can you hear the rustling of leaves? The chirping of birds? Try to identify each distinct sound, letting it calm your mind.

- **Touch:** Feel the earth beneath your feet, the texture of a tree's bark, or the breeze on your skin. Use your sense of touch to ground yourself in the present moment.
- **Taste:** If it is safe and appropriate, taste something from nature—perhaps a leaf of mint or a piece of fruit. Let this remind you of nature's ability to nourish your body and mind.

1. **Reflect:** After you have engaged all your senses, sit quietly for a moment and reflect on how this experience made you feel. Do you feel calmer, more focused, or more connected to the world around you? Take a moment to journal your reflections, capturing any insights that come up.

Practicing Mindfulness in Nature

Mindfulness is about being fully present—aware of your surroundings, your senses, and your body. Our minds are often racing, seemingly on autopilot, and full of thoughts that drain our energy. But where we place our attention is where we give our power. When we shift our focus to our body or our senses, the mind quiets.

Nature is an ideal environment for practicing mindfulness. Leave behind all distractions—your phone, social media, and to-do lists. Instead, engage all your senses. Notice the different shades of green in the leaves, the scent of the air, and the songs of the birds. Allow nature to teach you the art of presence, and feel your consciousness rise as you immerse yourself in the moment.

10

Reconnecting with Nature—Realigning with Self

"In every moment with nature, you receive far more than you think."
—Nicole Reina, Author, Facilitator, and Mindset Coach

N ow, it is time to experience nature in a way you may never have before. As you prepare to engage with the journaling prompts ahead, consider setting aside a moment today—whether 15 minutes or several hours—to consciously connect with the outdoors. Whether you visit a park, take a mindful walk, or sit quietly in a natural space, know that every moment spent intentionally in nature is a powerful investment in your health, consciousness, and overall well-being.

Remember, the key to manifestation is not just found in the Law of Attraction or in changing your thoughts. As you learned in Chapter 9, the true key is elevating your consciousness. This shift changes the frequency of your thoughts—not the thoughts themselves. At each level of consciousness comes an entirely new perspective, offering fresh groups of thoughts. When you shift upward in consciousness, you gain access to higher thoughts, better ideas, and experience less resistance.

Nature helps eliminate resistance by giving the mind a place to rest. In nature, distractions are minimal—only beauty surrounds you. As you take time to appreciate this beauty and express gratitude, your consciousness naturally rises. What once confused you may suddenly become clear. You might gain insights or ideas about challenges you face, or simply find peace amidst the bustle of daily life.

Journaling Prompts

1. Observe the Flow of Nature: Take a moment to observe how nature flows effortlessly without resistance—how the wind moves the trees, or how water flows around obstacles.

- What areas of your life feel like they are resisting the natural flow?
- How can you practice more acceptance and let go of control?

Write your thoughts.

_____

_____

_____

_____

_____

_____

_____

_____

_____

_____

_____

_____

_____

_____

_____

_____

2. Connection to Nature Mirrors the Connection to Self: As you sit in nature, reflect on how connected you feel to your surroundings. Take a moment to take three deep breaths to ground yourself and clear your mind, then answer these questions:

- What does this sense of connection (or lack of connection) reveal about how you relate to yourself and others?
- How can you deepen your connection to both?

Write your thoughts.

_____

_____

_____

_____

_____

_____

_____

_____

_____

_____

_____

_____

_____

_____

_____

_____

_____

_____

_____

_____

_____

_____

_____

_____

_____

_____

_____

_____

3. Simplicity: Nature thrives in simplicity, yet remains endlessly abundant. When we simplify our own lives, we clear away the mental clutter that holds us back, allowing space for true abundance to flow. As our inner world fills with peace, joy, and calm, our outer world begins to reflect this abundance in every aspect.

- How can you simplify your life to create space for more clarity and peace?
- What habits, thoughts, or relationships are no longer serving you and could be released?

Take a moment now to reflect and write your thoughts.

_____

_____

_____

_____

_____

_____

_____

_____

_____

_____

_____

_____

_____

_____

_____

_____

_____

_____

_____

_____

4. The Power of Stillness: Nature is full of life, yet often it is still. Take a moment to sit still as you reflect on the following questions. Before beginning, allow yourself to take three deep breaths to relax and clear your mind:

- How does sitting in this stillness affect your inner world?
- What thoughts or emotions rise to the surface when you allow yourself to be still?
- How can embracing more stillness help you shift your perspective to more love?

Write your thoughts.

_____

_____

_____

_____

_____

_____

_____

_____

_____

_____

_____

_____

_____

_____

_____

_____

_____

_____

_____

5. Releasing Old Patterns: Just as trees shed their leaves in the fall, we must learn to let go of old beliefs and habits to grow. Up until now, you may have written thoughts and feelings or emotions that you need to release. Make the decision now that you will release these thoughts for the highest good of all.

Remember, to let go of any thought or belief, all that is required is a simple intention to release it. You might say something like, "I release all thoughts and beliefs that no longer serve my highest good, allowing space for peace, clarity, and growth."

- Take a moment to write down the thoughts, beliefs, or habits you have identified that no longer serve you and that you are ready to release. Remember, holding on to anything that does not serve you creates resistance and prevents you from elevating your consciousness.

_____

_____

_____

_____

_____

_____

_____

_____

_____

_____

_____

_____

_____

_____

_____

_____

_____

_____

_____

6. Gratitude is one of the highest vibrational emotions we can experience, and it serves as a powerful gateway to joy and enlightenment. When we express gratitude—whether for something small or profound—we align ourselves with the energy of love, which naturally attracts more good into our lives. In moments of negativity or low energy, the fastest way to shift our vibration is to choose to pause and reflect on what we are grateful for.

- Reflect on something in nature that captures your attention—a tree, a bird, the sound of wind. What feelings arise as you focus on it with gratitude?
- How does the act of expressing gratitude elevate your current emotional state?
- How can you incorporate more gratitude into your daily life to raise your consciousness?
- Write down 10 things you are most grateful for.

_____

_____

_____

_____

_____

_____

_____
_____
_____
_____
_____
_____
_____
_____
_____
_____
_____
_____
_____
_____

7. Energy and Vibration: As we vibrate, we attract. Now that you have released old patterns and practiced gratitude, take a moment to tune in to how you feel.

- What emotions are present? How does your energy feel—grounded, peaceful, or scattered?
- How does your energy feel—grounded, peaceful, or scattered?
- Looking ahead, consider what practices you could incorporate into your daily life to shift your energy and better align with the frequency of nature, elevating your consciousness. It might be sitting still each morning or evening, taking a mindful walk, spending more time in the park, or journaling. The possibilities are endless, so have fun and get creative!

_____
_____
_____
_____
_____
_____

_____
_____
_____
_____
_____
_____
_____
_____
_____
_____
_____
_____
_____
_____
_____
_____
_____
_____
_____
_____
_____
_____
_____
_____
_____
_____
_____
_____
_____
_____
_____
_____

11

Conclusion

"When you create your life from a highly conscious place, you will find that things come to you from a magical space."
-Mike Connor, Author, Consciousness Coach, and founder of Attracting Grace

A s we reach the end of this journey, it is clear that the Law of Attraction is only a fraction of the equation in manifesting your desires. Many people have embraced its principles, only to end up frustrated and discouraged, wondering why their dreams are always out of reach. Perhaps they taste some of their dreams, just to have it snatched away. The human experience is challenging, and it requires a higher truth to truly survive and thrive. This book has revealed what has been missing: the essential role of consciousness in creation.

To truly harness the power of the Law of Attraction, you must go beyond mere positive thinking. You must align every layer of your conscious being with the life you wish to manifest. Since your consciousness is made up of three parts—the super-conscious awareness, the self-conscious thoughts, and the unconscious beliefs—it is not enough to want something; you must become it on every level.

You must embody your desired outcome to manifest it. You must "Be it to See it." Consistently visualizing and expressing the emotions of the end result will get you there.

By elevating your consciousness, you unlock the power to transform your life from the inside out. This process involves confronting the hidden fears and limiting beliefs that have been holding you back. Beyond just offering deeper insights, this book equips you with practical tools, including muscle testing and Dr. David Hawkins' emotional frequency scale, to help you measure your current state and make intentional shifts. With these tools, you can train your unconscious mind to see your dreams not merely as possibilities, but as inevitable realities.

The journey to creating the life you desire is not without challenges. I have faced plenty of them myself, but in the end, the challenges are worth it. They make life exciting and give it purpose. We are meant to be joyful, creative beings, not merely surviving. However, this journey is not for everyone. It is for those who are courageous—those willing to look deep within and confront the less pleasant parts of themselves.

It requires you to embrace all parts of yourself, even the uncomfortable emotions that arise from the depths of your unconscious. It is most certainly challenging, but doable. I know that if I can do this and be successful, anyone can. It is in this process of self-discovery and vibrational alignment that true transformation occurs.

The Support System: A Vital Need

A support system is crucial in undertaking this journey. It can be scary, but it does not have to be. When you have the right group of people supporting you and guiding you, it transforms the life you dream of so much easier. Should you decide to be courageous and move forward, become comfortable with change, as it is inevitable. Remember, like attracts like, so when your vibration changes, what no longer serves you will change. Your environment will most certainly change as you adapt to your new vibration. Find a tribe that elevates you, supports you, and is there for you when the times are hard.

For the last several years, my tribe has continued to be those in Attracting Grace (Attractinggrace.com), a group that was developed to assist others in growing their levels of consciousness. It is because of this group that I have been able to withstand the trials and tribulations that come with the changing of consciousness. They have supported me, loved me, and held space for me while I grew and manifested my desires. Without them and their esteemed founder and my mentor, Mike Connor, I would not be living the life I live today. Without them, I would not have experienced the miracle of reversing my profound hearing loss. I am grateful for the knowledge I gained and am grateful for the new me.

Now, it is your turn. Will you join me in raising the consciousness of humanity and creating a better world?

The power to create lies within you. Remember, the Law of Attraction alone is incomplete, and much of the information out there can be misleading. Trust your body's intelligence and use muscle testing to discern truth from falsehood. With the knowledge and tools provided in this book, you now hold the missing key to fully unlocking your manifesting power. Finally, you can break free from the hamster wheel of life and empower yourself to become a real creator. You are not a passive recipient of fate; you are the full creator of your reality.

Your dreams are not just within reach—they are already yours, waiting for you to step into alignment with them. As you move forward, carry this truth with you: your consciousness is your most powerful tool. Use it with intention, and watch as the life you have always dreamed of unfolds before your eyes.

Now, it is time to take the next step. Emotionally Visualize your dreams into reality. Do the work and let your unconscious do the rest. The world is ready for the new reality you are about to create. So go ahead—unlock your full potential, align with your desires, and manifest the life you have always known you were meant to live. You deserve the best life, and it is finally within your reach. After all, it is only you vs you.

I sincerely hope you have enjoyed this book. It has been an honor to write it, and even more of an honor to have been courageous enough to put it out to the world.

This is Part 1 of a 2-part series of why the Law of Attraction is incomplete. Part 2 deals with focus and sustaining momentum, where I provide insight on how to stay focused when life throws you curve balls. I will also provide a journal to help keep track of your growth in measuring the levels of consciousness, with an area for notes and ideas to help you stay on track to creating a life you love. You are in for a treat—Stay tuned!

Remember, challenges are inevitable. It is how you rise that matters.

Now, the time is yours. Step into your power and create the life you deserve.

*****

Final Thoughts, Ideas, Clarity, and/or Insights

When we raise our consciousness, new thoughts may start bubbling up more frequently into our awareness. Remember, consciousness naturally ebbs and flows, like the tides of the ocean. This fluctuation explains why we sometimes "forget" what we were thinking. In some cases, it may be due to short-term memory; in others, it simply reflects a shift in our level of consciousness. We can only access thoughts that align with our current level of awareness.

After reading this book and completing the exercises, your consciousness has likely expanded. In the coming days and beyond, pay close attention to the new thoughts that arise. As they come to you, take a moment to write them down for reflection later. Use the following pages to journal these thoughts or choose your personal journal—whichever feels right for you.

_____

_____

_____

_____

_____

_____

CONCLUSION

CONCLUSION

Thank You

"To help raise one person's consciousness means you have helped elevate the whole of humanity." — Nicole Reina

Dear Reader,

From the bottom of my heart, thank you for taking the time to read *The Law of Attraction is Incomplete, Part I: How to Leverage Consciousness to Unlock Your Manifesting Power.* I hope that the insights shared within these pages have touched your life in a meaningful way, just as they have profoundly shaped my own journey.

Life's path can often feel unpredictable, even overwhelming, but if this book has helped you navigate its challenges with more clarity, peace, or purpose, then my highest intention has been fulfilled.

If this message has resonated with you, I would be deeply grateful if you could share your thoughts in a review on Amazon or Google. I read each one personally, as your feedback not only fills me with joy but also guides me in refining my future works.

Thank you, dear reader, for your love, your trust, and for joining me in raising the consciousness of our world, one heart and mind at a time.

With love, light, and much gratitude,

Nicole Reina

About the Author

Nicole Reina is a beacon of resilience and empowerment, transforming adversity into a powerful source of inspiration. Despite being orally deaf with just 2% hearing, Nicole has never allowed her challenges to define her. An award-winning business owner since 2017, she took a bold step in 2022 to become a Mindset Coach, dedicated to helping women entrepreneurs unlock their true potential. She is also a certified John Maxwell speaker, trainer, and facilitator.

Nicole's journey is nothing short of miraculous. Through the very techniques she teaches, she has reversed her profound hearing loss by over 20%, defying what was once deemed impossible. Her mission is clear: to empower others to step into their power, embrace their inner genius, and create the lives they have always dreamed of, rather than settling for a life by default.

Nicole's coaching style is transformative, shifting perspectives to cultivate clarity, ease, and joyful creation. Her passion for personal growth and consciousness education shines through in every speaking engagement, workshop, and private session she leads.

Beyond her professional pursuits, Nicole finds joy in the simple pleasures of life. Whether she is immersed in a book, sketching her thoughts, meditating, or hiking through the serene forests of North and South Carolina, she carries a deep sense of gratitude and purpose. She lives in Tega Cay, SC and treasures the moments spent with her husband John, their two children Alex and Catalina, and their beloved Cocker Spaniel, living each day with intention, purpose, and love.

Nicole Reina's story is a testament to the extraordinary power of the human spirit. If she can achieve the impossible, imagine what you can do.

CONTACT INFO:

To learn more about Nicole and to follow her work, check out her website at iamnicolereina.com.

Follow her on social media:
YouTube: @iamnicolereina
Instagram: @iamnicolereina
LinkedIn: Nicole Shults Reina

Bibliography

1. Lipton, B. H. (2012). *The Biology of Belief: unleashing the power of consciousness, matter & miracles.* Retrieved August 26, 2024, from https://www.tachyon-aanbieding.eu/Documentation/The%20Biology%20of%20Belief.pdf.

2. Say, J., & Say, J. (2020b, August 15). 57 Steve Maraboli quotes on life (LOVE YOURSELF). *Gracious Quotes.* https://graciousquotes.com/steve-maraboli/

3. Neumann, K. D. (2024, February 20). *What Is The Law Of Attraction? – Forbes Health.* Forbes. Retrieved August 27, 2024, from https://www.forbes.com/health/mind/what-is-law-of-attraction-loa/.

4. *Matthew effect.* (n.d.). Wikipedia. Retrieved August 27, 2024, from https://en.wikipedia.org/wiki/Matthew_effect.

5. *Matthew 25:29.* (n.d.). Bible Hub. Retrieved August 27, 2024, from https://biblehub.com/matthew/25-29.htm.

6. Byrne, R. (Producer). (2006). *The Secret* [Film]. Prime Video.

7. Winfrey, O. (Host). (2007, February 16). *The Secret* [TV episode]. In *The Oprah Winfrey Show.* Harpo Productions.

8. Dispenza, J. (2012). *Breaking the Habit of being Yourself: How to lose your mind and create a new one.* Retrieved 18 August, 2024, from https://openlibrary.org/books/OL25078846M/Breaking_the_habit_of_being_yourself.

9. Allyn, R. (2022, February 23). *The Important Difference Between Emotions and Feelings.* Psychology Today. Retrieved August 28, 2024, from http://www.psychologytoday.com/us/blog/the-pleasure-is-all-you

rs/202202/the-important-difference-between-emotions-and-feelings

10. *The Roots of Emotional Intelligence.* (n.d.). Psychology Today. Retrieved August 28, 2024, from http://www.psychologytoday.com/us/basics/emo tional-intelligence

11. Dimas, J. (2020, January 24). *72 Inspiring Abraham Hicks Quotes To Get You Into the Vortex.* - Dwell in Magic®. Retrieved August 28, 2024, from https://jessicadimas.com/abraham-hicks-quotes-that-will-turn-your-life-around/.

12. Blias, O. (2021, June 6). *Your subconscious mind creates 95% of your life.* Thrive Global. Retrieved August 27, 2024, from https://community.thriv eglobal.com/your-subconscious-mind-creates-95-of-your-life/

13. Hawkins, D. R. (2020). *The Map of Consciousness Explained: A Proven Energy Scale to Actualize Your Ultimate Potential.* Hay House.

14. Hawkins, D. R. (2016). *The Eye of the I: From Which Nothing Is Hidden.* Hay House.

15. Hawkins, D. R. (2014). *I: Reality and Subjectivity.* Hay House.

16. Hawkins, D. R. (1998). *Power Versus Force: An Anatomy of Consciousness: the Hidden Determinants of Human Behavior.* Veritas.

17. Schucman, H. (2012). *A Course In Miracles.* White Crow Books.

18. McTaggart, L. (2017). *The Power of Eight: Harnessing the Miraculous Energies of a Small Group to Heal Others, Your Life, and the World.* Atria Books.

19. Hay, L. (1988). *Heal Your Body: The Mental Causes for Physical Illness and the Metaphysical Way to Overcome Them.* Hay House.

20. *Carl Jung on the Unconscious and Dreams.* (2015, April 6). Academy of Ideas. Retrieved August 27, 2024, from https://academyofideas.com/201 5/04/carl-jung-on-the-unconscious-and-dreams/.

21. Shults, Sharla Lee. Dancing With the Earth. 2024. Self-Published.

Made in the USA
Columbia, SC
25 November 2024

47193766R00070